Leading Technological Change

The Cambridge Educational Management series

This series for educational managers focuses on key topics of current or emerging interest in the field of ELT, providing readers with an understanding of theoretical concepts, examples of these concepts in action and practical ideas for implementation. For more information on these titles, please visit: www.cambridge.org/elt

Other titles in this series:

Cultivating Teacher Wellbeing

Kate Brierton and Christina Gkonou

Promoting Professional Learning

Silvana Richardson

Leading Technological Change

Andy Hockley
Lenise Butler

CAMBRIDGE
UNIVERSITY PRESS

University Printing House, Cambridge CB2 8BS, United Kingdom

One Liberty Plaza, 20th Floor, New York, NY 10006, USA

477 Williamstown Road, Port Melbourne, VIC 3207, Australia

314–321, 3rd Floor, Plot 3, Splendor Forum, Jasola District Centre, New Delhi – 110025, India

103 Penang Road, #05–06/07, Visioncrest Commercial, Singapore 238467

Cambridge University Press is part of the University of Cambridge.

It furthers the University's mission by disseminating knowledge in the pursuit of
education, learning and research at the highest international levels of excellence.

www.cambridge.org
Information on this title: www.cambridge.org/9781108744300

First published 2022

20 19 18 17 16 15 14 13 12 11 10 9 8 7 6 5 4 3 2 1

Printed in Great Britain by CPI Group (UK) Ltd, Croydon CR0 4YY

A catalogue record for this publication is available from the British Library

ISBN 978-1-10874430-0 Paperback
ISBN 978-1-10874427-0 eBook

Table of Contents

Acknowledgements

The authors and publishers acknowledge the following sources of copyright material and are grateful for the permissions granted. While every effort has been made, it has not always been possible to identify the sources of all the material used, or to trace all copyright holders. If any omissions are brought to our notice, we will be happy to include the appropriate acknowledgements on reprinting and in the next update to the digital edition, as applicable.

Chapter 1: Figure adapted from Serrat, O. (2017) Appreciative Inquiry. In: *Knowledge Solutions*. Springer, Singapore. https://doi.org/10.1007/978-981-10-0983-9_63. Copyright © 2017 Springer, Singapore. Reprinted by permission from Springer via Copyright Clearance Center; Force field analysis taken from Defining the 'field at a given time.' by Lewin, K. (1943). *Psychological Review, 50*(3), 292–310. https://doi.org/10.1037/h0062738. The content is in the public domain; Copyright © Dan Martin. Reproduced with kind permission; Copyright © Marino Komlusan. Reproduced with kind permission; **Chapter 2:** Copyright © Simon Schubert. Reproduced with kind permission; Figure taken from *Diffusion of Innovations,* 5E by Everett M. Rogers. Copyright © 1995, 2003 by Everett M. Rogers. Copyright © 1962, 1971, 1983 by Free Press. Reprinted with the permission of The Free Press, a division of Simon & Schuster, Inc. All rights reserved; Triple E Framework by Professor Liz Kolb. Copyright © Triple E Framework. Licensed for re-use with attribution under CC BY 4.0; Gartner 'Understanding Gartner's Hype Cycles', Philip Dawson, Alexander Linden, Keith Guttridge, Katell Thielemann, Nick Jones, Jackie Fenn, 2 July 2021. Reproduced with kind permission; SAMR Model reproduced by kind permission of Ruben R. Puentedura; **Chapter 3:** Grid taken from Project management templates from Project Agency. Copyright © 2008 Project Agency. Reproduced with kind permission of Ron Rosenhead; The J-Curve by David Viney. Copyright © 2003-2020 David Viney. Licensed for re-use with attribution under CC BY 4.0; Dr James Welsh for the adapted text from 'Technology Integration Matrix' by Dr James Welsh. Copyright © 2019 Florida Center for Instructional Technology. Reproduced with kind permission of Dr James Welsh; **Chapter 4:** Bloomsbury Publishing Plc for the text taken from © Martin Wedell, 2009, 'Planning for Educational Change: Putting people and their contexts first', Bloomsbury Publishing Plc. Reproduced with permission; Copyright © David Oakley. Reproduced with kind permission; Diagram adapted from Dr John Kotter's 8-steps process model for leading change. Dr Glenn Hole, Associate Professor at Molde University College. Reproduced with kind permission; Summary of Dr John Kotter's 8 Steps taken from *Leading Change* by John Paul Kotter. Copyright © 1996 Harvard Business School Press. Reproduced with permission; Gibbs reflective cycle taken from *Learning by Doing: A guide to teaching and learning methods* by Graham Gibbs.

Thanks

The authors would like to thank those people who contributed greatly in the creation of this book: Jo Timerick and Karen Momber at Cambridge University Press; Gordon Lewis for his advice and suggestions as we wrote; Graham Skerritt, our amazing editor, who contributed a huge amount to the book; Dan Martin, David Oakley and Simon Schubert for allowing us to use abridged versions of their case studies (which they originally wrote as students on the International Diploma in Language Teaching Management); and Josip Sobin of Jantar–IH Split for the case study in the Conclusion.

Andy: Thanks to all those people who have worked with me along the way, and especially Donald, Ron, Christine, George, Steve, Jenny, Lucie, Banu, Martyn and Silvana, who are and have been colleagues, mentors and friends. Thanks to Erika, Bogi and Paula, who thanks to the pandemic had to share a small space with me while we all worked on our various projects – school, university, work, this book – and bore my occasional stress with good grace and patience. And of course, to Lenise.

Lenise: To all of you who have worked with me and believed in me in my career, studies and while exploring new pursuits, you have gotten me here. Thank you, Gordon, Mark, Leon, Courtney: colleagues, mentors and examples to follow. To my amazing Coordinators and Directors on my teams, you've helped me build my experience to be the leader I can be today. To my family, my motor and my inspiration to do better every day. Raul, Mathias Daniel (Stinky Face), and my Kaden Boy, LOS AMO. And of course, my mom, who has always been my biggest fan. Thank you, Penny, you were right.

Preface

The Cambridge Educational Management series is intended to support academic managers in dealing with key aspects of their role. The books in the series are designed to bring together theory and practice, providing insights into key parts of the academic manager's role.

Clearly, academic managers have many things that they need to deal with, to the point where it can often seem overwhelming responding to all the urgent (yet not necessarily important) things that we have to be on top of. But, from time to time, we must make space to look forward and plan rather than simply react, and this is particularly important when dealing with technological change.

A large language school in Latin America that I once worked with learned this lesson the hard way when replacing all its cassette players and VHS video machines with integrated TV/DVD units which could also play audio CDs. Teachers and students were very excited by this (at the time) extremely modern approach. The flaw in the change model was only discovered on the first day back at school, when they realised that while the technology had been updated, the materials in the staffroom were still only available on cassette and VHS.

While technological change is not new, as demonstrated by the story above, the pace of development seems much faster now. We as a profession are dealing with new apps, classroom technologies, translation software, virtual learning environments and so on all the time, with new possibilities opening up frequently (and sometimes disappearing equally rapidly). Attend any language learning conference and the exhibitors' area is dominated by technology. Sometimes it can feel that education and educational change are being driven by technology, rather than the other way around. It's important that academic managers can stand back and take a look at the bigger picture, ensuring that decisions regarding technology are made from the point of view of need and value to the organisation, its staff, teachers, and students.

It's hard to imagine that there is any language teaching organisation that hasn't undergone some form of change connected to technology over the past two decades. I've worked for and with a number of institutions, all of which have added new technology-based elements to their programmes over that time. In some cases, this has been relatively smooth and effective, and in others it has caused a number of problems, many of which could have been foreseen. New technology, whether it be hardware or software, usually involves a purchase, and in some cases, this is as far as the managers making the purchases have looked, and have overlooked the need for support (both technical support and ongoing training support for users). This seems to be one of the most common issues, with the other major one being decisions made by the wrong people and for the wrong reasons.

This book will help you avoid these kinds of problems when implementing technological change. By presenting a model for change and providing clear guidance for each step of the way, you can, when your institution next decides that change is needed, ensure that the process by which that change is carried out is more effective and inclusive.

Andy Hockley, Series Editor

About the authors

The authors are both highly experienced academic managers, and have worked in many contexts and with many different organisations around the world.

Andy Hockley has been involved in ELT for over 30 years, as teacher, trainer, manager, and management trainer. He co-authored *From Teacher to Manager* (CUP, 2008) and *Managing Education in the Digital Age* (The Round, 2014) and also wrote *Educational Management* (Polirom, 2007). He currently works as Academic Director for the Bell Teacher Training Campus, as global lead trainer for the International Diploma in Language Teaching Management, and as MA Tutor for NILE / University of Chichester on the Management in Language Education part of the MA in Professional Development for Language Education. He lives in deepest Transylvania.

Lenise Butler has been an educational leader, based in Mexico, for many years. Among the positions she has held through this time have been Global Director for Languages with Laureate International Universities, National Director of Languages with Universidad del Valle de Mexico, and Director of the International Center for students at the Universidad Anáhuac México Sur. She has a Master in Education with a focus on bilingual education, and is currently finishing her dissertation for an Ed.D. in Leadership in International Education. She is passionate about the effective use of technology in language teaching and learning. Lenise is also mother to two boys and is working on putting theory into practice in raising bilingual, bicultural kids.

Introduction

About this book

We are very aware of how challenging and all-consuming the management of a language teaching organisation (LTO) or programme can be. This is true whatever the type of organisation or the department you are responsible for, whether it be a university department, a private language school, a non-profit adult education provider, a state school department, or some other educational institution. With all that you have to deal with, the thought of starting out on a process of major technological change may very well be a daunting one. When your first question is "Where do we start?", it can be easy to find yourself a little stuck.

The objective of this book is to help you understand the many options that exist and to set your LTO on the road to effective technological change. We'll guide you through the process of asking the right questions, filtering the differing advice and suggestions, and supporting your team in making the change.

The process of writing and developing this book has coincided with the global Covid-19 pandemic and all that this has entailed in the world, and particularly in our profession. Clearly, there has been a great deal of enforced technological change that has come about through this, and we'll look at this in the conclusion to this book. While the pandemic has forced many of us to take steps toward online, blended, or hybrid learning, perhaps before we have felt entirely prepared, this book will help you move forward no matter where your courses and programmes are along the spectrum of technology use. Looking at the change management strategy of integrating technology (or enhancing the technology that already exists) into an LTO's programmes, no matter what stage of implementation you may be at, can provide you with a base to create long-lasting positive change.

We hope that this handbook will be useful and supportive as you move forward and develop new ways of working and new ways of supporting student learning.

Technological change in language education

All successful organisations need to be prepared for change. Technology develops, global and local economies go through transition and evolution, and the theories and approaches that guide ways of working evolve. In all of this ongoing development, there is a need for organisational agility and readiness to respond to differing circumstances. This reality does not simply apply to technology firms, but to all industries, including education. It is said we live in a business environment characterised by "VUCA" – volatility, uncertainty, complexity, ambiguity (Bennett and Lemoine, 2014), and in such an environment being inflexible and slow to adapt can be fatal for an organisation's stability.

LTOs are no exception, whether they be university departments, private language schools, state sector K-12 departments, training divisions at large companies, refugee resettlement programmes, vocational training centres, educational foundations, or any other educational institution or company. The successful ones will demonstrate the ability to adapt, be resilient in changing circumstances, and be ready to take important decisions. It is not just the owner or executive director of such an organisation who needs to be ready to make these decisions – academic directors, language programme coordinators/directors, and heads of administration also need to be alert to and aware of the trends and changes in their sector, and to be thinking about what changes would suit their needs and the needs of those that they serve.

The source of the most obvious changes in our profession over at least the last decade, and undoubtedly for the one to come, is technology. Technological development creates new levels of customer expectation and empowerment, including for more personalised learning, greater flexibility in class scheduling, support for administrative and academic course activities, advances aimed at improving learner autonomy, self-study and more. In addition, social media channels open up greater levels of feedback and opportunities for a collective voice, which in turn can build demand, stimulate change, and also affect reputations.

The development of technology in the education sector can feel like it is accelerating. From our experience of talking to academic managers and other managers and leaders in the language teaching industry, the pace of change can occasionally seem overwhelming. In some cases, this results in a kind of passive decision-making process, whereby new technological solutions (whether in the classroom or the office) are introduced either through simply following the competition or through bowing to the demands of others. The purpose of this book is to support managers and leaders in making informed decisions on technological innovation in their context, based on pedagogic criteria as well as general need. The idea is to re-empower managers to feel able to make decisions based on useful information and through the consultation of key stakeholders – most of whom will be end users of the technology chosen.

You may be asking yourself whether this book is about managing change or about evaluating technological solutions. The simple answer is that it is about both. A more in-depth response is that this book is fundamentally a book about the management of change in the education sector, with a focus on technological change. We discuss the technological needs of language programmes and advise on how you can make decisions on technological innovation or supplementation, with the goal of helping managers to implement the change from the beginning (identifying needs and potential options) to the end (incorporating the new technology into "business as usual"), but with the understanding that this process of change and adaptation is ongoing and that there will likely never be a moment when some technological change is not taking place. It is worth noting that the approach we have taken is intentionally to recognise that technology will continue to evolve, and the needs of the programme will as well. As such, the change model we discuss is intended to guide managers and stakeholders in the LTO during the process of change, and provide tools to help you evaluate technology, but does not focus on specific technology innovations or assume that any set of options may be the most desirable. Rather, the tools will help you find tailored solutions which best fit each circumstance.

This book is a practical handbook in building the conditions for successful change. It aims to help organisations make well-informed decisions, effectively implement these decisions, and sustain and evaluate the changes. As a result, the overall structure of the book relates to the fundamental processes that must be dealt with in tandem in order to successfully choose, introduce, develop, maintain and re-evaluate technological change in LTOs.

What is educational technology?

Educational technology is a broad, and arguably meaningless, term in itself. It covers a number of quite different innovations and possibilities which a language programme might consider as an enhancement of what they are currently doing. Broadly speaking, these can be divided into a number of categories:

1. The first of these, and possibly the one that most people think of as 'educational technology', is technologies that are designed to facilitate and enhance learning and the learning experience. These tools may

be used in the classroom to augment or even redefine the traditional approach to learning and teaching, or they may be intended to improve learning beyond the classroom, such as in blended or flipped approaches to learning, or they may be used for distance education programmes.

2. A second category is that of assessment, finding ways that technology can be used to more effectively measure student learning and also to release skilled people from the often repetitive and routine task of marking. Somewhat connected to this latter rationale are other advances which free teachers up from time-consuming and tedious tasks, allowing them to focus on more purposeful and meaningful work, thereby increasing motivation.

3. The third category includes the kinds of software or hardware which have been developed to improve the systems of administration, such as stand-alone financial management, student record keeping, or timetabling software, as well as integrated school management systems which can support all the tasks of language programme administration, including, in some cases, classroom functionality as well.

4. A final category of technology we can find increasingly in use in the educational setting is technologies that have not been created with educational purposes in mind, but which have become vehicles for activities and learning within the classroom and learning programmes. These can include social media, software and technologies related to administration or other career areas being incorporated into the classroom, as well as communication technologies being increasingly used to facilitate online learning.

| Core beliefs behind this book

We approach this handbook with a set of beliefs and principles that underpin and shape our thinking.

Organisational goals. It is fundamentally important to keep in mind what exactly it is that your programme exists to do. By doing this when planning and making change, we start with the aspiration and the goal, and then deal with the obstacles and potential limitations, rather than the other way around. It is of course true that we cannot do everything we might want to, for various reasons. However, fundamentally our role, and the philosophy of this book, is to imagine what might be possible and then see whether it can realistically be achieved. Approaching innovation in this way ensures the sort of creative thinking that allows educators and educational leaders to consider the best-fit solution to fulfil the need. This in turn leads to better-informed results, a bank of information, and possible innovations that can be harnessed for future areas of opportunity, rather than starting from the question, "How much money do we have spare in the budget?" and moving from there.

People. Central to any organisation, and to all changes of whatever nature, are people. People are the instigators of change, people are the implementers of change, and people are the beneficiaries (we hope) of change. Change requires people to adapt and engage. For this reason, this book will focus to a large part on people – on communication, on relationships, on dealing with resistance, and on motivation, among other "soft skills".

The value of educational technology. Educational institutions and language teaching organisations must respond to the needs of current language learners, which includes the need to develop what are often referred to as 21st century skills (Keane, Keane and Blicblau, 2016). Technology is often at the core of how such skills are addressed for students who are increasingly more in tune with the use of technology in all aspects of their daily lives. Useful and successful innovation within educational technology is focussed on making the learning experience more personalised and interactive, on providing more scaffolded support for teaching and learning for student and teacher, on providing more effective solutions for assessment of learning, and on streamlining or simplifying the processes of school administration or the daily tasks of all staff in the language programme.

A critical approach to technology. While institutions, employees, students, and other stakeholders are often able to see how the use of technology can create a real benefit to the programme, students and learning outcomes, it is not a simple question to understand exactly *which* technology should be used, nor is it entirely clear how institutions can choose that technology and ensure best fit for the programme or model. Additionally, in a learning environment where the choice of technologies may seem unlimited, and the pressure to provide the best to students overwhelming, it can be difficult for educational leaders to avoid what Buckingham (2007: viii) called "a superficial infatuation with technology for its own sake". In short, a culture of critical thinking about technology and its role in education must exist. This will be highlighted several times during the chapters that follow, as the integration of technology into LTOs and programmes must be accompanied by real analysis of the benefits and challenges, and with a realistic perspective on how much the technology will add to the programme. We aim to share questions and tools that will provide the basis for a holistic evaluation of technology, and that also serve as a reminder for managers and stakeholders that no technology can replace strong programme foundations and personalised programme solutions.

The structure of this book

This book has been written with a focus on practice, with the backbone of theory which will guide managers through the process of working within their specific programme needs in their own settings. Practical application is covered, which will help readers create a real proposal for managing the integration of technology in their own language teaching situations.

Within each chapter, readers will find case studies bringing alive the context and process. These authentic cases illustrate and provide context to the ideas outlined. Case studies are drawn from the authors' own experiences and from their extensive networks of colleagues and fellow professionals in the industry.

The chapters in the book will follow the basic stages of change as mapped out in Figure 0.1.

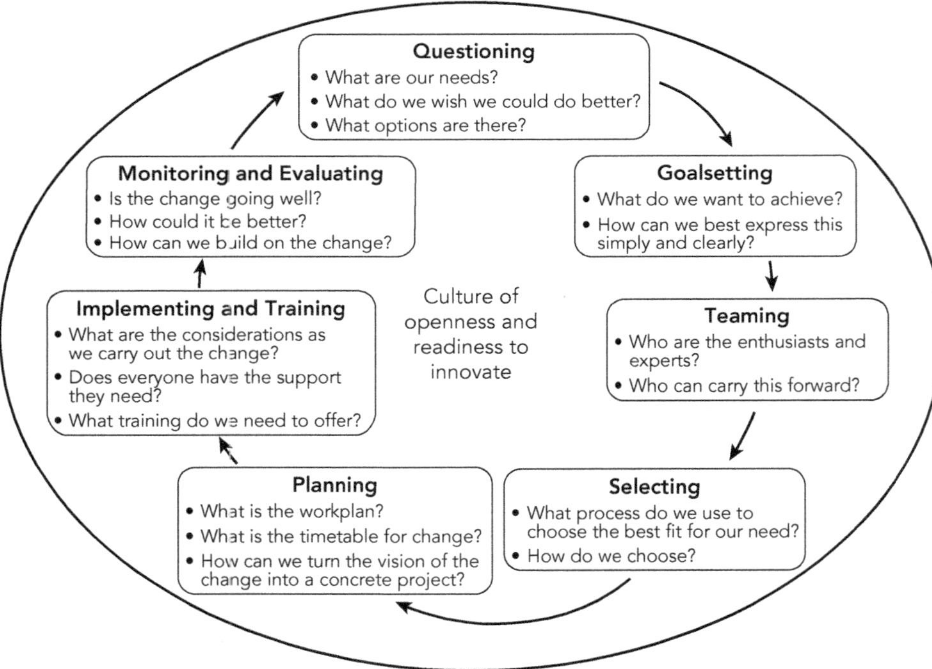

Figure 0.1: The stages of technological change

These stages of the process of technological change will be integrated through the book with change management and project management principles, to provide a blueprint which can be applied to any such transformation, combining local context with theory.

A brief overview of each chapter can be found below:

This **Introduction** defines the principles and approaches that the rest of the book is founded upon.

Chapter 1: Preparing for innovation begins by outlining the way that an organisation might promote a culture that is open to innovation and which gives staff a sense that they can suggest and promote new ideas and approaches – the context described in Figure 0.1 as a culture of openness and readiness to innovate. Subsequently, it looks at the beginning of the process of change: the Questioning and Goalsetting parts of the cycle. We look at where the motivation for change comes from, and how it can be channelled and focussed. We also address the key questions of need and applicability of technology in addressing the gaps the organisation has identified. We propose the setting of goals to both provide direction and present a clear message to staff and other people who will be involved in making the change come about.

Chapter 2: Creating a team of navigators outlines the next stage in the process of change, Teaming. We describe the process by which a team of key people are formed and can begin to work together to navigate the process of bringing about the change. We consider how technological innovations can be evaluated and analysed to meet the goal we have set, and then use the SELECT model to choose the best tool for the need.

Chapter 3: Planning the change focuses initially on the key elements involved in the planning of change. We introduce a project management approach to ensuring that the process of transition is clear and well thought through. Thereafter we provide guidance on implementing the change itself. This chapter also includes thoughts on managing resistance to change and how to engage in ongoing communication during the change process. We describe the importance of supporting end users as they deal with the challenges inherent in working with unfamiliar technology. This also includes the creation of ongoing training and support programmes, ensuring that everyone who needs to interact with the new technology is included and their needs responded to.

Chapter 4: Monitoring and sustaining change addresses the critical phase of ensuring that the change continues to be appropriately managed and monitored over time. The success of any programme, and any change within that programme, is contingent on consistent, careful review, as well as continuous contact, training and motivation for all those involved to continue moving toward its success. The topics addressed in this chapter include:

ongoing support and necessary adjustments; maintenance/upgrade and other procedures; ensuring successes are celebrated; a team approach to ensuring support is given where needed; documenting and recording best practices; and building on the success of the change. In addition, we think about the process of re-evaluation of our innovation.

The **Conclusion** provides a summary of the process of change described in this book.

The **Appendices** offer a set of checklists and other tools designed to be of value in the process of building technological change in language teaching organisations.

(See **Appendix 1** for an overview of the stages of technological change.)

1 Preparing for innovation

This chapter:

- considers the organisational culture that is desirable to lead change
- looks at ways of questioning the status quo, from SWOT analysis to appreciative inquiry
- explains the various sources of change, whether they be top down, bottom up or from somewhere else
- outlines how to set motivating and clear goals

Introduction

This chapter will look at the first two stages of the model of change (see Figure 1.1 below): Questioning and Goalsetting.

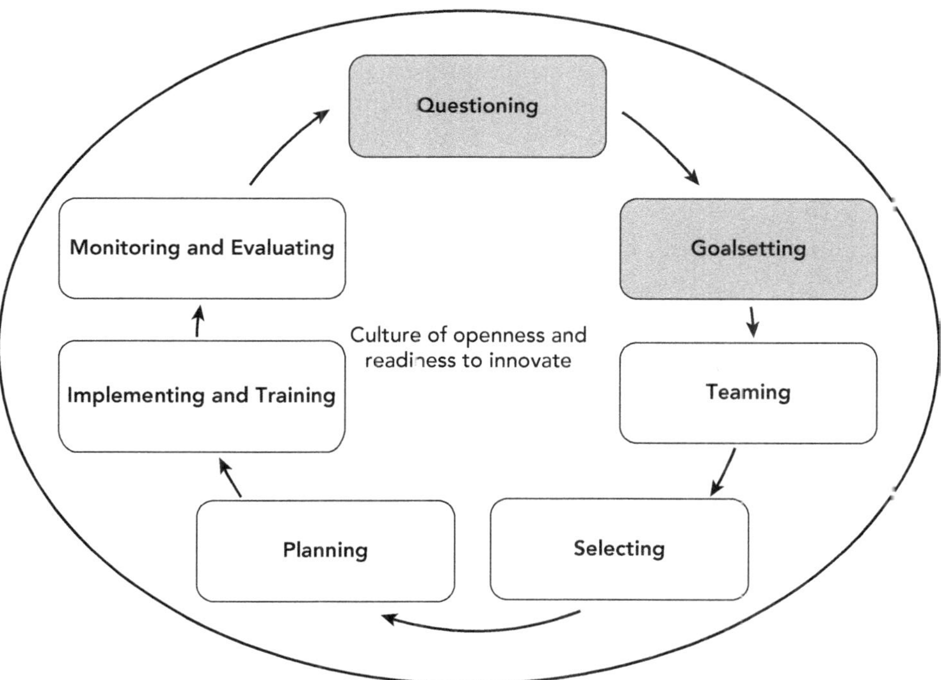

Figure 1.1: The stages of technological change

A culture of openness – creating the conditions for change

In our model of **the stages of technological change** (see Figure 1.1), the environment in which change is best supported is described as a "culture of openness and readiness to innovate". Before explaining the different stages of the cycle, it is important to outline what we mean by this, since it is arguably the foundation of successful technological change.

You may have worked for an organisation (educational or otherwise) in which people were engaged and enthusiastic, and there was a genuine sense of community and togetherness – an organisation where people felt listened to and valued, and as a result were prepared to invest their time and energy into the work they were doing... and beyond it. It's also possible you have worked for the opposite – an organisation in which people came in, worked through their hours, didn't rock the boat, and remained indifferent to how the organisation progressed. It is the first of these organisations that we are aiming for.

An outsider visiting such a language teaching organisation would see a collaborative staffroom – people sharing positive stories from the classroom, asking for help ("Anyone have any great activities to go along with Module 4 in this coursebook?"), and offering suggestions. They would also notice a sense of collaboration between teachers and support staff – teachers respecting the importance of the work done by the office staff, and doing what they could to support that work – and vice versa. The academic manager's door would be open, and she may be seen around the school, chatting to students, available to teachers between lessons, and generally ensuring things were running well.

This is the kind of school culture in which a teacher, say, might approach a manager with something she read in a journal about ways of better engaging students with technology; or in which a group of office staff might come together and think about what would make their job more productive. In short, it is an organisational culture in which change is ready to emerge, organically.

Culture, however, is difficult to change quickly. Management writers have, for decades, been looking at approaches that can be used to create a more engaged and positive organisational culture. For example, in 1990, Peter Senge posited the idea of the Learning Organisation, and at the time of writing much attention is focussed on the **Agile organisation** (see panel below). In all of these models, a set of management practices are suggested as ways of making the culture more open and engaged – from teamwork to professional development to effective leadership.

We will cover many of these areas as we work through our model of change, in this and subsequent chapters, but one which deserves special mention at this stage is effective leadership.

Arguably this whole book is about good leadership, but in summary, what we see as good leadership is that which facilitates and fosters openness and questioning. A good leader listens to and trusts those professionals (educators and others) 'under' her in the organisation. This form of leadership is sometimes referred to as **Servant leadership**, and we would recommend readers who wish to explore this idea further to take a look at the works of Greenleaf (2002), Spears (1998), and Iarocci (2017), amongst others.

Effective leadership also involves developing a clear **vision** and **strategy** – the vision of a collaborative organisation is clearly understood and shared by everyone, which is to say, it is one that staff buy into. The most obvious way to create a truly shared vision is to create it together. It's not a corporate branding exercise, rather a clear statement of what everyone wants to achieve. Such a statement can then be used in focussing and bringing a critical approach to every proposal or goalsetting exercise (see later in this chapter).

A 2018 report by the New Zealand government's Education Review Office (ERO), *Leading Innovative Learning in New Zealand Schools*, outlines why we need to be open to transformation and innovation in supporting 21st century learners. ERO's research found that successful innovative school leaders:

- are proactive in working with the whole-school community to develop a strong, future-focussed vision for their school
- ensure the vision has learner outcomes at its centre
- are well-informed so that decisions build on best practice for 21st-century learners
- have a growth mindset – are supportive of experimentation
- quickly address elements of strategy if those elements are not working
- develop a school culture of continuous improvement to support the vision
- maintain coherence across all domains of the school, aligning everything to the vision
- are effective change managers, able to take staff with them on the improvement journey through timely professional development and good communication

🔑 Agile

A lot is written these days about the 'Agile organisation'. As this idea covers much of what we mean by the "culture of openness and readiness to innovate" from our stages of technological change model, it is worth providing a brief overview of what this 'agility' refers to.

The idea of Agile dates back to 2001, when a group of software developers coined the term as an approach to iterative project management in software development. Since then, the idea has slowly expanded and been applied to other management/organisation areas. Now much larger than project management, it is closer to a model for how organisations can be adaptable and resistant in a VUCA (volatile, uncertain, complex, ambiguous) world. It is in many ways tied closely to the ideas of change and transition (and is presented as a way that organisations can be open and ready for change). It would be fair to say, however, that it is a collection of ideas that have been combined and repackaged as Agile.

Broadly speaking, Agile involves a focus on the following areas:

- teamwork
- engaged employees
- open and transparent communication
- frequent and active communication
- clear vision and strategy
- effective leadership

In the model we propose in this book, you will see that these are the keys to our approach to handling the change. It is this idea of an agile working culture that we see as being at the heart of an organisation which is successfully adaptable.

🧠 Task 1.1: How Agile are you?

For each statement, give your organisation or department a score out of 10, where 10 means that this happens most of the time, 5 means that it happens only about half the time, and 1 means that this happens very seldom.

1. People are encouraged to give honest feedback in my organisation (and feel willing to give it). ___

2. Teachers and others are encouraged to develop and grow personally and professionally. ___

3. Staff see management as supportive and encouraging, and willing to listen to new ideas. ___

4. We have regular meetings and discussions to look at what we do, to see if we can improve on the courses or services that we offer. Strategic planning is something that happens with the involvement of all staff. ____

5. We have a clear, worthwhile and agreed-upon vision (which we all share and understand) for our LTO that we use to guide our actions. ____

6. The managers of this LTO reward, recognise, and encourage learning (for individuals and teams). ____

7. We regularly look outside our own LTO to see if there are new ways, procedures or approaches we can use to improve the way we do things. ____

8. When problems occur, teams are formed (or already exist), who then look into solving or dealing with that problem. ____

9. Much of the work we do (e.g. curriculum development, assessment, new courses) is done in teams. ____

10. People are encouraged to question and challenge assumptions and mindsets, and to come up with innovative new ways of doing things. ____

Total score: ____________

SCORING

- **80 and above:** Your organisation seems to already be Agile and possess a culture of openness.

- **60–79:** You have made steps towards an Agile culture but can improve in some areas.

- **40–59:** Your organisation has a few of these positive qualities that are necessary in an Agile culture, but has a long way to go.

- **Less than 40:** Your organisation is a long way from having an Agile, open culture.

Now, think about ways that you could improve your score. What specific actions can you take?

Stage 1: Questioning

In many traditional models of organisational change, innovation is generated by managers and leaders. However, increasingly, these traditional models are less applicable to institutions working with new and evolving models of education, in which teachers and other stakeholders take on a more proactive or fundamental role in the institution. At the same time, new technologies and expanded methodologies in LTOs involve the student deeper in the learning experience than the traditional learner role may have dictated in the past. Rather, students are now involved in decisions around how and when to use technology and held responsible for the outcomes technology contributes to, and as a result they hold progressively more influence in the way in which institutions evolve and grow.

All organisations must be constantly open to changes in the professional environment and they must be organised in such a way as to be able to act upon the ideas they identify as relevant areas of opportunity or possible ways in which they will change or grow. Due to the participatory nature of educational environments, this must be true of people at all levels within the organisation.

In the case of technological innovations in particular, with the accelerating pace of development and new additions to the educational technology environment taking on new importance, the idea of leader-led change, where only one or a small group of individuals holding a position of authority are able to sift through all of the possible options in order to choose the correct one, is simply unworkable.

Given the above and given the fact that it is those on the front line, or 'at the chalkface', who will have a clearer idea of what tools might support their students' learning, and those working in the administration side of the organisation who will likely have a clearer picture of what is needed to streamline student record keeping, for example, it must be our aim to foster the culture outlined above in which all employees are genuinely engaged. This engagement implies that they will be encouraged not simply to "do their jobs", but also to be constantly in a state of questioning and imagining what would improve the teaching/learning experience or other workplace practice. Along with this engagement in the organisation itself must come a similar engagement in their profession. It is through such commitment that ideas and creative inputs into the work of the LTO can surface.

However, having said all of this, it is also key to look at things with an eye to perceiving them in an asset-based way, as opposed to a deficit-focussed approach. We have a tendency to look only at the gaps in what is present in our working environment (the deficits), rather than starting from what we actually have (the assets).

On a basic level, a simple **SWOT analysis** (see panel below) can ensure that we are as aware of our strengths as of our weaknesses. A SWOT analysis is a technique used in the early stages of planning or decision-making, providing a framework for analysing the current situation. SWOT stands for Strengths, Weaknesses, Opportunities and Threats, and can be used to analyse these four aspects of your project, department or business as a whole.

⚷ Conducting a SWOT analysis

As mentioned above, a SWOT analysis is a tool to help analyse a situation and create a picture of some of the issues around a potential change. To conduct one, you make notes in a grid like this:

Table 1.1: A SWOT analysis grid

Strengths	Weaknesses
Opportunities	Threats

When completing a SWOT analysis, the following questions can act as a useful guide:

Strengths

- What do you do well in this area?
- What resources do you have?
- What advantages do you have?
- What do other people see as your strengths?
- What do students/clients see as good in this area?

Weaknesses

- What could you improve?
- Where do you have fewer resources than others?
- What do others see as your weaknesses?
- What are the bottlenecks or inefficiencies in the way things are now?

Opportunities

- What opportunities can you see?
- What trends could you take advantage of?
- Are there new technologies that you could use in this situation?
- How can you turn your strengths into opportunities?

Threats

- What threats could harm you?
- What are your competitors doing?

- What is changing in your working environment?
- What threats do your weaknesses expose you to?
- What will happen if you do nothing to change the way things are now?

Table 1.2 below is an example of a completed SWOT analysis grid for an LTO that is looking at the way student reports and grade sheets are currently generated.

Table 1.2: Example SWOT analysis grid

Strengths	Weaknesses
- Everything functions reasonably well. - Systems and procedures are effective. - Response time to student enquiries is on average one day. - Information provided to teachers is up to date.	- All responses to enquiries come in form of printouts. - Data for teachers is also printed out. - If Joanna is off work, nobody else can generate the report. - On a few occasions, response time has been four days. In one case, it was a whole week. - If teachers have not submitted all the relevant information in time, up-to-date reports cannot be generated. - Takes time and staff could be better engaged doing other tasks.
Opportunities	Threats
- Reports could be generated and delivered to a mobile phone. - Students and teachers could have an app. - Process could be speeded up and made paperless. - Other staff could be trained, so system is not reliant on one or two individuals. - Having own school app may look appealing to customers. - Frees up staff for more strategic tasks.	- Some competitors already do this. - Goal is to be as paperless as possible, and not doing this will go against that goal. - Increasingly, customers want instant responses. - Risk being left behind.

While a SWOT analysis is a great way to start, it is wise to go even further, and develop a clear picture of what we can build from, rather than what seems to be missing. An example could be a private language school in which students are broadly satisfied with the teaching and the environment in which it takes place, to the point where they are enthusiastic about homework and working on their English outside of the classroom. This positive foundation could be supplemented with the addition of some form of Virtual Learning Environment (VLE) which students can use to access extra resources and materials and interact, asynchronously, in their free time.

Approaching the situation in this appreciative way makes it clear to all that their work and commitment is recognised and valued (whereas a more deficit-focussed approach might lead them to feel like all that is noticed is that which is not functioning well).

This approach is known as **appreciative inquiry**, and in their book *Switch*, Chip and Dan Heath (Heath and Heath, 2011) refer to it as "bright spots". They suggest we ask the question, "What's working right now and how can we do more of it?"

⚷ The 4D Cycle

An appreciative inquiry approach to looking at change is often outlined in something called the **4D Cycle**.

1. **Discovery**
   "What's already working?" Identify the processes and approaches that are going well. This is the appreciative part of appreciative inquiry, looking at the positive, and using it as a starting point from which to build.

2. **Dream**
   "What might be?" What do you wish we could do better, or more effectively? This is what much of this chapter has described as a questioning approach. Ask yourselves what the programme's goals should be (these may relate to your LTO's overall strategic plan). Perhaps identify a couple of areas that could be developed. Envision what the situation would look like if you could achieve what you've thought about here.

3. **Design**
   Come up with a plan. You've identified where you are (discover) and where you want to go (dream), so now the question is how you get there from

here. Brainstorm ideas and possibilities. Build links and connections. This, broadly, covers much of the next two parts of our stages of technological change cycle: Goalsetting and Teaming.

4. **Deliver** (also called 'Destiny' or 'Deploy' in some versions of the 4D Cycle) This is the realisation phase. Put into practice what you decided upon in the previous stage. This is the stage referred to as "Implementing and Training" in our model. Try things out and evaluate to see what works. Experiment as much as is possible.

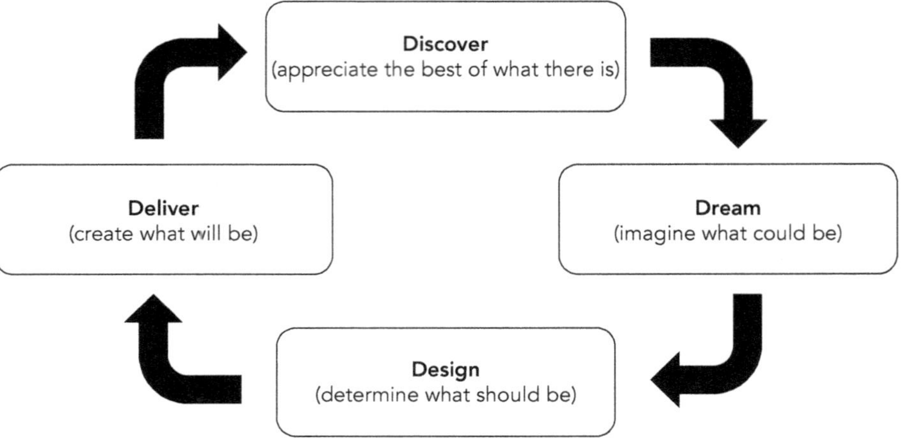

Figure 1.2: The 4D Cycle

🧠 Task 1.2: Applying the 4D Cycle to your LTO

Try out the 4D Cycle for yourself. Take one area of work in your LTO – perhaps teaching, or assessment, or some of your office processes – and apply these questions:

1. What about this area works really well? Can you identify the specific parts of this area in which things work successfully and effectively?

2. Looking forward one year, what would you like this area of work to look like? Imagine someone coming to visit your school and you showing them the things you were really proud of. What would they be? Are there some areas which you'd really like to develop from where they are now, building on what is there already?

3. How do you get there from here? What would need to happen to achieve the ideal you pictured in question 2? Are there some clear, concrete steps you could take? What's the first step?

4. Do it! And then, after you've had a chance to implement these changes, go back to question 1 and start again.

Fitting into the wider context

The place of change in the overall strategy

LTO managers are often primarily concerned about the *practicalities* of implementation, which is understandable, as this is where so many of us have experience and expertise, and we are therefore very aware of the practical issues of running an academic programme. We tend to move quickly (in our thought processes at least) from "This sounds like a good idea" to "OK, what do we need to think about and how can we make this happen?" However, we must also bear in mind the bigger picture – where our programme fits into the wider organisation (if there is one) and where we fit into the overall organisational strategy, as well, of course, as being clear about our own objectives in the introduction of the technology.

Long-range planning and creating a strategy

Strategic planning is an extremely important element of leadership. It is possible that many LTO managers have never been involved in this process as it may be carried out at a 'higher' level in the organisation. However, in situations of managing change, whether the academic manager has ever been involved in setting strategy or not, the process requires leaders to think about how the programme will affect the experience of students, staff, faculty and others in the organisation, as well as the overall outcomes of the programme. Every educational organisation should have a vision which underpins and guides its programmes, the institution, and what it provides to the students.

It is not the remit of this book to look into the nuts and bolts of long-range planning, but it is important that any change you plan fits in with the **long-range plan** (LRP).

Planning for success

LRPs need to be taken into close consideration when planning for operational success and implementation. While operational and implementation planning is by nature very detailed and meticulous, without holding the overall vision for the programme, it is often easy to get side-tracked by the intricacies of operations and lose track of the big picture, which can be fundamental in providing input when making difficult decisions. It is possible (sometimes even probable) that managers are forced to decide between priorities or placement of resources, and timelines and rollouts can be affected. Knowledge of the big picture can provide guidance when sacrifices need to be made to keep things on track. It will also help you make your case with those who hold the purse strings if you have used the LRP as a starting point and a guide for your planned change.

An **operational plan** is derived from the organisational **strategic plan** and should provide a detailed action plan with which you intend to accomplish the objectives of the programme. It should outline who is responsible for each element – tasks, timeframes, cost (including ongoing costs) and targets (often referred to as Key Performance Indicators or KPIs), which will be benchmarks to measure the success of the project. You may find that templates for operational planning already exist within your organisation. If so, using these formats makes it easier for other departments to understand your documents and facilitates communication with other stakeholders. If your organisation does not have its own templates, many can be found online and adapted to your specific programme or project. We will return to the details of planning – in the context of the change proposed – later in the book.

A language school strategic plan will likely have a number of sections, covering areas such as engagement, student achievement, and wellbeing, incorporating in-depth targets and plans for the three to five years ahead. Hopefully, the academic department has been involved in the creation of the plan, but even if not, this plan needs to provide guidance and direction for the actions you choose to take. It is important, therefore, that any change, such as the ones described in this book, complements the strategic or long-range plan. In short, you need to act within the guidance laid out in the strategic plan, and also need to convince those above you that what you propose fits in with that plan.

The sources of change

Bottom-up change

Staff (both teaching and administrative) should be encouraged and supported to keep up to date with the latest developments in their profession. It may not be economically viable to send large numbers of teachers to international conferences to investigate the latest ideas or tech-based approaches. However, the academic manager can ensure that teachers have access to journals and articles, along with a well-structured and bottom-up professional development system, which in turn will allow them to be up to date and at the cutting edge of thinking about their profession, while at the same time allowing managers to help track progress.

Bottom-up **professional development** (PD) (also known as teacher-driven teacher learning) programmes are referred to as such because the teachers themselves are involved in the decisions around the kinds of professional development that will be most valuable for them to engage in. Correctly implemented, the teacher in such a PD programme participates in the organisation, practice and follow-up of their own development opportunities. The role of leadership in this type of PD for staff and faculty in an LTO is to ensure the development pathway is achievable and relevant to the development and direction of the institution itself, and also to track and support teacher progress and follow-up through the programme.

Teachers being direct participants in the development element of their profession allows them to become part of the process of change in a much more proactive manner. They are allowed the space and tools in which to evaluate their own performance in light of the institutional need, and help identify training or PD opportunities that might contribute to the change needed. In this way, they can imagine how certain innovations in classroom practice could be adapted in their context to enhance the student experience.

The role of the manager here will be to support staff to develop their own inquiries into their profession. This could happen through the performance management process or simply as a meeting to think about what forms of professional development would be of interest – and to make it clear that this is not about a one-size-fits-all approach, but a way for teachers, for example, to form small groups who wish to investigate what it is about teaching and learning that interests them and how they might enhance what is currently being done.

From the classroom perspective, for example, it is imperative for teachers to be thinking, "What is it that I wish we could do here? What would support my students' learning? What would make my job as a teacher easier?" These kinds of questions can be a catalyst for teachers to begin to form their own professional communities, often referred to as **communities of practice**, in which they can come together (in person or virtually) to share their ideas around topics of mutual interest. Often, these communities of practice are born from the need to find solutions to problems or areas of opportunity they see in their practice and in their institutions.

These kinds of self-organising communities of practice (as per Wenger, 1998) come together over a common interest and a mutual desire to work on a specific domain of knowledge. They are fuelled by the fact that they are a community which is united by common interest, in turn providing motivation and support, as well as a willingness to share ideas. But they are not simply discussion groups – they are motivated by a desire to change or develop their practice.

Like-minded teachers coming together to see if they can locate or imagine a solution to issues of student learning in an intentional manner strengthens their presence on campus, and provides a forum for other teachers to learn from their experiences. Reading about how other teachers in other contexts have addressed the same or similar issues can lead to a sharing of best practice on a wider scale and can promote the formation of **professional**

learning networks (PLNs) with teachers with similar interests. This type of network can move beyond the institutional and face-to-face level of the direct community and expand through social media or other virtual means.

Promoting this type of interaction within the institution promotes the kind of organisational culture that will generate ideas and thoughts which will strengthen the bottom-up approach to improvement and moving forward. Some of the ideas and proposals from professional learning communities will involve technology and others will not, but the key is to develop the space and to provide the conditions to ensure that the suggestions that emerge are given the chance to be developed – and also challenged.

To follow on from the last point, it is, of course, extremely important that **critical thinking** be incorporated during this bottom-up approach. The shiny newness of some technology can blind us to thinking about it in an in-depth way. "Wouldn't it be cool if all the students in my class had a tablet?" is not a good starting point for building useful innovation. However, "In what ways could I improve my students' learning and give them more confidence in the use of the target language?" followed by, "Is there a tool that can support my idea here?" is likely to be a much more successful question. If teachers and others can be encouraged to first think deeply and critically about what they wish they could do in order to make the work of the organisation better, and then to see if there is some kind of already available concrete solution to that wish, then the culture of the programme has effectively allowed real, valuable, effective innovation to bubble up. Professional learning communities are one way in which these questions can be addressed. Ensuring teachers and other stakeholders in the learning environment approach these questions with the appropriate focus is a challenge that must be continually supported by the institution. There can be a temptation to follow a tech trend that we must be aware of, in order to ensure the technology is not just an add-on but rather really does address the issue. And if technology is *not* the answer to the specific problem, that also needs to become part of the culture of discussion and problem-solving.

Eventually, having thought through the different aspects of the innovation they see as desirable, adapting and implementing it to the specific context, teachers and other stakeholders will be ready to propose it to the academic manager (if it is the kind of change that needs approval).

Change from elsewhere

While it is possible, even desirable, that the drive for change will come from the bottom up, there will also, of course, be times when the motivation comes from elsewhere. Perhaps the marketing department are hearing from agents that schools that incorporate a certain technological innovation in their classes are attracting more students; perhaps the head office of a chain of schools requires that all their branches install some new student tracking software; or perhaps students hear of a new or improved global English test which has been moved entirely online, and therefore results are received more quickly. In these cases, it may be that managers and leaders will need to encourage the adoption of the necessary change. In the case of bottom-up change, it may be *managers* who need to be convinced, but with this kind of change it may be *staff* who exhibit resistance.

Kotter (1996) refers to the need to create a sense of urgency in starting the change process. That is to say it is worth thinking through different options to convince those who need to "unfreeze" (Lewin, 1947, cited in Cummings, Bridgman and Brown, 2015) – whether they be teachers, admin staff, managers, or any combination thereof – of the need to do so. Find ways to open a dialogue about what is possible or what competitors are doing or simply what you (or others) have learned through reading articles or attending conferences or discussing with colleagues in other institutions (through your PLN). Look into opportunities that could be exploited, areas where you are currently dissatisfied with a situation, and possible threats to your business in the future, and raise these as part of your discussion of the issue.

One way to understand where the energy for change is most strongly felt and to determine if the change is indeed one worth proposing is a tool called a **force field analysis** (see panel below). Another useful tool is presented in **Appendix 2**.

⚷ Force field analysis

A force field analysis (Lewin, 1943) allows us to assign a value or a weight to each of the factors influencing the current environment. Having done the exercise of listing and assigning a value to each, the model allows for readjusting or re-aligning values, depending on the outcome and perceived need for change.

We start by listing the forces which are pushing change. For example, some of the forces in the case of promoting an in-classroom technology change may include:

- student pressure (often found in the form of discontent or resistance to 'old' technology, lack of interest, or even students finding other ways to complete activities)

- teacher desire to try out new ideas or new techniques
- market forces (e.g. competitors are already ahead of us on this, and as a result they may be more attractive to potential students)
- publishers – materials are increasingly created with digital components (online supplementary materials, interactive whiteboard resources, etc.)
- out-of-date technology
- informed teacher belief that the technology in question will genuinely support learning

On the other hand, forces opposing change might include:

- cost
- concern that the new technology might turn out to be an expensive fad
- disruption
- staff fear/resistance (see below and Chapter 3)
- lack of interest in the language programmes themselves (or perceived lack of interest)

As can be seen, this example has elements of bottom-up change as well as externally-driven change.

To perform a force field analysis, assign each of the factors a weight and see whether there is a strong imperative to carry out the change you're thinking of. For example, in the diagram below (Figure 1.3), four factors are encouraging change: pressure from teachers and students, market need, the increasing amount of published materials using the technology, and the fact that the current system is obsolete. On the other hand, three factors are opposing the change: cost, teacher fear and potential disruption.

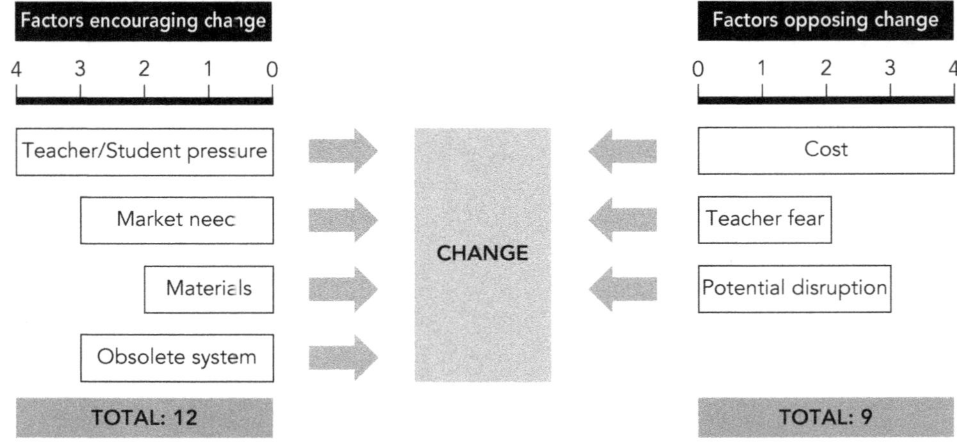

Figure 1.3: Example of force field analysis (Lewin, 1943)

Having completed the analysis, you can use it to decide whether or not to move forward with the decision or possible change. However, you can also use it as a basis for thinking about which forces encouraging change you can strengthen and which opposing forces you can reduce, in order to make the change more effective and desirable. For example, looking at the diagram above, teacher fear could be overcome with training; this might reduce the weight of that fear by 2 (while adding 1 to the overall cost). Alternatively, an argument could be made that the downward effect on student numbers of not having updated technology in the classroom is such that it reduces the effective cost of change; this is another way in which the urgency to change could be influenced.

Unpopular change

There are, of course, times when unpopular change from elsewhere is pushed upon us – whether this be from a wider organisational requirement institutional change, or some other imperative. An example of such a change, in the technological area, is the change of a software package on the grounds of security: a new VLE (Virtual Learning Environment, a web-based platform which provides resources and materials as well as activities and interactions) or LMS (Learning Management System, a software application used in the educational setting for the management, administration, tracking and documenting of courses) might be imposed upon you because the wider institution in which you work has decided that there are more secure options which make sense at a corporate level – regardless of the upheaval or challenge that this would cause for teachers and students alike.

If you believe that a change will make life more difficult for your team, the first step to approach the situation is to ensure you have all your facts ready and argue your opposition with the people in authority as strongly as possible. Often proposing an alternative solution that you believe to be a better option can be a strong persuasive tactic. However, if this approach fails, and you are left with the need to manage this change, then it is your role to do everything that you can to make it as successful as possible. The temptation, of course, will be to side with your team and present the change as an unfortunate reality (e.g. by saying "I agree that it's a terrible idea, but sadly we have no choice"). As problematic as making the change successful may already be, this is guaranteed to make it even more difficult. Your role as a leader in change is ultimately to support the change and manage it in the best possible manner, putting a positive face on it, which will support the transition for teachers and staff and ultimately facilitate success during the process.

The better way to deal with such a situation is to start with the positives. Think through the change that you are being asked to manage and find which pieces of it will be valuable and useful. Perhaps work with a couple of key people within your department who will be able to help with looking into the positives, while also thinking through the obstacles. Connect the change to your organisational values or mission. How does this change support our overall goal and what it is we do here? Then plan your communication with the wider team. How will you communicate, what will you communicate, and when? The ideal way of communicating anything unpopular is at a face-to-face meeting, however daunting that might be, as soon as the decision to implement the change has been made. When communicating this change, bear the following in mind:

- prepare what you need to say (but don't wait)
- give specific and detailed information (don't be vague)
- think to yourself: "What would I want to know if I was in their shoes?"
- give people time to vent (but be clear that there isn't a debate)
- describe the positives
- outline what has to be accomplished and by when
- ask for volunteers to form a team (or several teams) to work on the change
- respect those who resist

(Further ideas about presenting information can be found in **Appendix 8**.)

Q Case study: Imposed unpopular change

Dan is the academic manager at a language school which is part of a large global chain. In 2017, the head office of the organisation decided that all teaching materials in all schools would be transferred to the cloud and that all the schools in the organisation would use Microsoft SharePoint. The initial response of teachers was fairly negative, with the primary reasons being the workload involved in transferring materials, and a lack of understanding as to why the change was necessary.

Dan met with teachers and they talked through the issues. This process was helped by the fact that the head office had not merely dictated the change, but had also given Dan clear reasons and a clear goal for the change. They explained that they wanted not only to improve the infrastructure of the digital operations, but also to provide more for the teachers in terms of resources and teaching tools, which would be much simpler and more effective with the cloud-based solution.

While Dan had reservations about the change, he realised that this also provided an opportunity. Materials and resources which had been built up over time within the school had become very difficult to navigate, with various documents stored seemingly haphazardly over the internal server. This change would force the academic department to sort through all the material and rationalise it considerably. During the meeting with teachers to talk about the change, he also raised this, and it was perceived by the staff as a clear benefit. In addition, he set up a system of regular meetings where the people tasked with transferring over the materials could raise issues that they had faced. Because these issues were addressed and, in some cases, passed on to head office for a response, there was a sense that while the change was not necessarily welcome, nor without issues, there was a clear goal and prompt responsiveness from management.

Change from the manager

While change can come from below, from outside (e.g. from market forces), or from above, it can also be instigated by you, the manager. Perhaps you have seen a gap in what it is you are offering or perhaps you have attended a conference and been impressed by a new piece of software. Having taken yourself through the same critical thought process outlined above in the bottom-up change process, the next step would be to bring in others. It is always worth having more than one person to evaluate an idea, so create a team of staff who would be potential users of the innovation and have them critically evaluate it too. Obviously, if you believe that staff may be unwilling to criticise or challenge an idea of yours, either because of organisational culture or of national culture, then you will need to find a way to create the space for this to happen. One possible approach would be to create an anonymous questionnaire, including questions such as the following:

1. What do you understand the planned technological innovation is designed to do?
2. From your understanding of the innovation, does it seem to be a good way of achieving this?
3. Would you be interested in being part of a team to take this forward? Why / Why not?

Working at a private college of English in South Australia, three teachers had recently taken professional development training courses through a local university. Much of the coursework had taken place through the university's VLE, and they realised that this could be a way for their own students to continue engaging with their coursework beyond the classroom. As most of the students at this LTO were on English for Academic Purposes or university pathway courses, the teachers felt that not only would this give students a chance to improve their English both outside and inside the classroom in a way which was likely to be engaging for them, but it would also prepare them better for their degree courses once they had moved on. Students would be able to communicate with each other out of the classroom, practise their writing skills and, at the same time, allow the teacher to monitor their interactions and language use.

Students were very active online and were fast to respond to notifications coming in on their phones. In addition, the school was attempting to cut down on photocopying for cost and environmental reasons. For these reasons, the idea to move activities and practice tasks onto an online platform seemed like a very good one.

The teachers sat down together and worked out what it was that they were doing currently that had the potential to be improved upon. They decided that they were not looking for a complete overhaul of the system, but rather a more dynamic approach that could find new ways of getting through the syllabus which made better use of the students' own resources and expertise.

They had a meeting to put down their ideas and discuss methodology. Together they uncovered a number of different applications and websites that could play a role in creating a more dynamic setup in their classrooms. They understood they could not change the curriculum but that they could alter how they presented it and how the students were to participate in it.

Management involvement was minimal. All three teachers understood that they had to work within the pedagogical framework that was set at the school for the academic courses. The work had to encompass the curriculum and it was to be presented to the students in a professional manner. The workload for the students was to remain the same. The style in which it was presented was one of the challenges from the teachers' side, while where to discuss ideas and where to get information inside as well as outside the classroom were the biggest challenges on the students' side.

They identified a number of potential software solutions, all of which were free in their basic form, so that they were able to try out the different options. Different teachers volunteered to trial the different platforms, and over the course of the trial period the benefits and limitations of the various options were discovered – from the perspective both of the students and of the teachers.

While the academic manager was kept informed, he decided to remain in purely a monitoring role. When the teachers (now not only the initial three instigators, but also the rest of the teaching body) had worked through the process to decide on a solution, taking into account student feedback and engagement as well as their own impressions and needs, they presented their preferred solution to him, and he was happy to support the solution they proposed, once he had satisfied himself that it didn't present any issues that the "change team" had overlooked, such as privacy and security.

 ## Task 1.3: The origins of change

Think about some recent changes that your department or programme has undergone. Where did they come from? Who instigated the change? Was it from a single source, or from more than one?

Stage 2: Goalsetting

Once it becomes clear that change is necessary and desirable, even though at this stage we might not know exactly what form the change will take, it is necessary to clarify the goal. Only with a clear goal will it be possible to work on the details of the change. The process of clarifying the goal will also ensure that all of the necessary critical thinking has gone into the intention.

Think through what the change is designed to achieve. What are the intended outcomes? What will things look like when the process of change is over? Crucially, *why* are we doing this? The goal will help you be clear what it is you want, what the innovation will achieve, and also how you will know what success looks like when you come to evaluate the change.

The initial goal needs to be clear but general and, importantly, memorable. This goal will form an essential part of the communication that will need to be undertaken to the various stakeholders involved in the change. A clear, concise statement of what the intended end result of the change is will not only help with the communication but can also be easily referred back to. A goal statement of this type might be, for example: "Our level tests will all be computer-based and automatically marked" or "The student tracking software, the finance software, and the timetabling software systems will be integrated."

One useful concept to think about here is the difference between 'change' and 'transition'. **Change**, as it is termed in this distinction, is the endpoint, the goal of the exercise. What we are trying to emphasise in this phase of the cycle is defining that change very clearly – what people can expect to see, what they can expect to be able to do at that point. **Transition**, however, is the process through which we will have to go to get from here to there. Arguably, in many change processes it is selling the change as vision which is much the easier task. As an example, moving to a new house can be envisioned and looked forward to. The endpoint of the change is (usually) desired and the benefits can be imagined. However, the actual transition process of getting to that point when we have finished moving, and all the other stages of the process prior to moving, is the hard work. This transition process will be discussed in the following two chapters.

 ## Task 1.4: Set a goal

Think about something you want to change. This could be something for yourself, or within your workplace. Can you create a clear and memorable goal, preferably in a single sentence? If not, why not? Rewrite it until you can. Then print it out (or write it out) and put it somewhere where you will be regularly reminded of it.

Summary

In this chapter we have looked at the organisational culture which will lend itself to a positive attitude towards change, as well as allowing creative ideas to come from various sources. We have then begun our change cycle with the idea of questioning – making sure that we ask the right questions to provoke and promote the change that will be successful for our LTO.

We have discussed several kinds of change and how they might be present within an LTO. It is important to note that change may be presented in one or many of the ways in which we have discussed. As managers, our primary role in dealing with change is to support the overall success of the institution. That means, as leaders in the change management process, we need to work toward positive implementation, even, occasionally with unpopular solutions.

Finally, we have turned these ideas and suggestions into clear and memorable goals, which will set the course for the rest of the process of introducing the change that will meet the needs we have identified.

 If you want to find out more…

Cooperrider, D. L., and Whitney, D. (2005). *Appreciative inquiry: A positive revolution in change*. Berrett-Koehler.

Cooperrider developed the idea of appreciative inquiry with Suresh Srivastra, and in this book, he and Diana Whitney expound upon the idea in a very accessible way.

Holbeche, L. (2018). *The Agile Organization* (2nd Edition). Kogan Page.

Linda Holbeche provides a thorough and clear guide to the concept of organisational agility, resilience and engagement, and how these ideas connect with innovation.

Kotter, J. P. (1996). *Leading Change*. Harvard Business School Press.

Possibly the seminal work on change management, Kotter presents an 8-step model for change, specifically aimed at the leadership of change, rather than its management.

Senge, P., Kleiner, A., Roberts, C., Ross, R., Roth, G., and Smith, B. (1999). *The dance of change: The challenges of sustaining momentum in learning organizations*. Doubleday.

Senge's work on the learning organisation is here developed into a set of ideas regarding how to lead and manage change. Described as a "resource book", it involves extensive case studies and examples.

Wenger-Traynor, E., and Wenger-Traynor, B. (2015). *Introduction to Communities of Practice*. Wenger–Traynor. https://wenger-trayner.com/introduction-to-communities-of-practice/

This freely available paper, from the developers of the idea of communities of practice, provides a clear and concise overview of the concept and the way it is used. It also provides links to other sources, should you wish to look further.

2 Creating a team of navigators

This chapter:

- considers the various issues involved in building a team to guide and lead the change
- describes ways that you can support and help the team to do their best work
- shows you how to break your goal down into SMARTER objectives
- highlights the most important aspects of initial communication regarding the change
- presents the SELECT model, designed to simplify and clarify the process of decision-making

Introduction

In the previous chapter we looked at the sources for change and how to question the status quo, as well as ways to set clear goals. In this chapter we will discuss more deeply how to build a team to take the change forward, as well as discuss a model you can use in the decision-making process of selecting technology for your LTO.

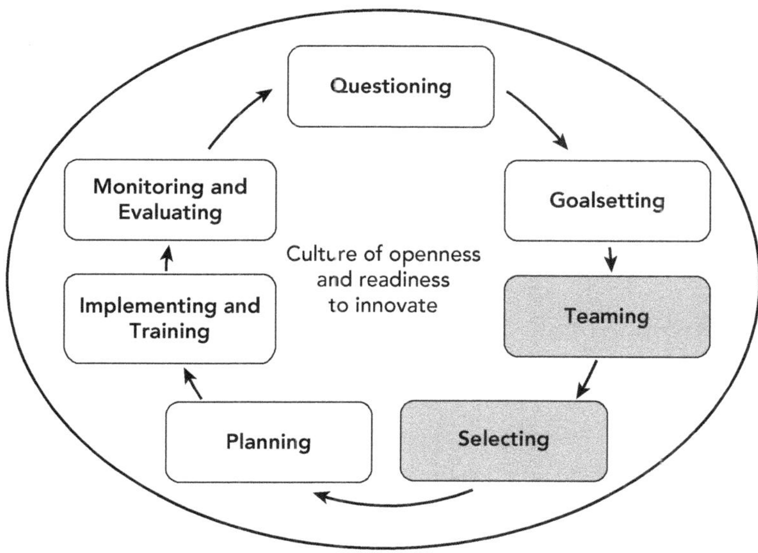

Figure 2.1: The stages of technological change

Stage 3: Teaming

After setting the goal, it's time to assemble the team that will push forward with the innovation. Kotter (1996) refers to this as "building a powerful coalition". However, unlike the suggestion inherent in Kotter's use of the word "powerful", in this instance it does not necessarily mean a coalition of the traditionally powerful in the organisation, the managers or people at the top of the organisational chart. Rather, the word 'powerful' refers to the combined influence of those who have arguably the most interest in the success of the change from the perspective of the end users – and of course in most of our cases, those end users will likely be teachers and students.

It may well be that you will need some key stakeholders from the management team in order to facilitate the change at the higher levels of the organisation, but it is crucial to bring people in who will be the genuine end users of the solution – some of the teaching staff, if it is a classroom-based (or online learning-based) change, or office staff if it is something that is likely to impact their jobs. Clearly, if the idea for the change has come from certain people, then it is those initiators themselves who will be key members of the team.

Other useful team members are those who can help "sell" the project – the types of people that Malcolm Gladwell refers to as "mavens" and "salespeople" (Gladwell, 2000). **Mavens** are those people who tend to accumulate knowledge and are delighted to share it (and are very good at sharing it), while **salespeople** are those who are excellent at persuading others by presenting ideas in such a way that others want to agree with them. Some teachers, for example, can be mavens. They are in a position to see the possibilities and opportunities from new classroom equipment, can look into what has already been tried, and imagine what benefit this would have to the programme. Such teachers are also able to transmit this enthusiasm and support to others. Getting these key people (mavens) on board is a major moment in getting the change off the ground.

Once you have a coalition of those mentioned above, this coalition, or at least a part of it, can become the initial project group – an actual, formalised, guiding coalition, who are given a remit to analyse the needs, investigate the possible solutions, and start planning the project.

Amy Edmondson (2012) uses the word "teaming" to highlight the fact that in the modern workplace, teams are rarely static contained entities, but instead are fluid and dynamic groups of people who frequently move in and out of various teams. In this instance, we would suggest something of a happy medium – teams that have a clear and fixed core group (as much as possible), with other people perhaps being brought in on a temporary basis as and when necessary and appropriate.

🧠 Task 2.1: Team formation

Think about the following questions and how you would answer, given your LTO context:

1. If you were hoping to develop a new system of online level tests, which five people on your staff would be the best to be on the team? Are the people you selected all teachers? Any front office staff? If not, why not?

2. If you were intending to refit the classrooms with projectors or similar, who would be your first choice for the team? (Again, choose five people.) Why these people? Between them, will they cover all the areas you need to think about (technological requirements, wiring issues, pedagogical usefulness, compatibility with other hardware, budget, maintenance, etc.)?

3. If you decided that you needed to buy some dedicated timetabling software which integrated with the student registration system, who would you most like to have on the team? Why?

Why work in teams?

Teamwork serves a number of purposes in an organisation:

1. Teams are greater than the sum of their parts. We've all had experiences where we've had half an idea and put it forward in a team and someone else has taken it and said, "Oh, yes, and if you did this…" and a third person refines it still further. If the first person in this example had been working alone, that idea would never have got off the ground. (Senge (1990) calls this "Team Learning".)

2. Creating teams allows you to build connections across the organisation. In the case of technological change, for example, the team might involve teachers, administrative staff, the IT department, and at least one member of the management team.

3. More people become involved with issues that matter to them. People have the chance to contribute rather than have decisions and changes imposed on them.

4. Change is much more effective when those affected by the change have been involved in creating it (as they would be if there was a team organised to drive the change).

5. It's a way of delegating tasks – giving staff opportunities to develop and giving you, the manager, more time to focus on other things.

How can teams work together most effectively?

Of course, working in teams requires very clear and constant management, and while this can certainly be complex and at times even burdensome (which is also completely normal), we feel that the benefits and strengths of working in teams are clearly worth the effort, and are, in fact, a crucial element of managing change and the integration of technology. Too often, LTO managers feel alone in their work, or are in a position where they are often required to do too much alone. Here is a clear opportunity to improve the results by working as a team.

There is a lot written about teams – about the roles people take on in teams (see Belbin (2010) for a starting point), about how teams develop and their lifecycle (e.g. Tuckman's famous "Forming-storming-norming-performing" model (Tuckman, 1965)), and much more. One such model, which we have found helpful in encouraging teams to work as effectively as possible, was developed by Teresa Amabile and Steven Kramer in *The Progress Principle* (2011).

The main idea behind their model is that people are more productive, more engaged, and more creative if they feel they are achieving something. In other words, they need to feel like they are getting somewhere. A good way to do this is by celebrating small victories along the path to completing the project. Amabile and Kramer suggest six mechanisms that managers can use in order to help their teams achieve these consistent small wins:

1. Set clear goals and objectives

Make sure that the goal of the team's work is very clear. Set objectives that ensure people understand the direction they are going in. When working with technology, for example, ensuring all the participants in the working group understand the need and where technology may fit, is crucial to avoiding the technology being chosen for other reasons. The objectives need to clearly include reference to where and how technology integration can be implemented. (Some example objectives will be found in the next section under 'Getting started'.)

2. Allow autonomy

While the goals have to be clear, teams (and their members) need to have the freedom to reach those goals in the way they think is best. The more control people have over their work, the more creative and empowered they will feel, and the more they'll recognise their own achievements. Don't micromanage! As long as the team has the right members in it, this should not be any kind of problem. For example, if there is someone from the IT department on the team, you can be sure that issues like security will be taken into account, while having teaching staff involved will ensure that the important pedagogical considerations are part of the team.

3. Provide resources

Make sure the team has what it needs to do the work they have been given.
If they don't have the resources, they will likely feel that the task itself is not
important. Resources include not only funding, or physical things like supplies
and technology, but training and support too, as well as access to the relevant
people and levels of clearance.

Other resources could include things like the chance to attend an educational
technology conference, or membership of a learning technologies group.
They could also involve being given access to test out the software options
being trialled.

4. Allow ample time

Give the team enough time to do the work (which will also allow them to be
creative). Deadlines which are too tight will result in lower quality work (and
less harmonious teams). However, deadlines which are too far off may also be
less motivating. So, coming up with deadlines which motivate but which do
not impede creativity and good quality work is important.

In most educational organisations, final deadlines tend to fit with the
academic cycle. For example, the installation of new equipment may take
place between semesters, or during times when classes are on a break for
other reasons. These points in the academic cycle provide a good starting
point for thinking about the various deadlines of a project. (See Chapter 3
for more on project planning and scheduling.)

5. Provide support and expertise

Make sure your team has access to support and expertise from outside the
team to help them progress with their work when they need it. As the manager,
this will likely include you, but it may also include others. Let these experts
know that they are expected to be available to help the team if called upon.
Ensuring your team also has access to the right people at the technology
providers whose products they are exploring is also crucial; as they test out new
ideas and think about how technology may be integrated, being able to ask
questions and explore limitations to each proposal is helpful, and will enable
your team to maximise their exploration and help ensure you are choosing
from the best possible options.

6. Help people learn from 'failure'

Sometimes teams don't succeed in reaching their goal. This may be because
they didn't work very well together, or it may be for reasons out of their control.

It's important to work with the team in understanding why things didn't go as planned and discuss what could have been done differently. If teams are punished for honest 'failure', the creativity and motivation in future work will be lost.

Let's say a team identifies some hardware which appears to meet the needs of the school very well. They devote some time to planning around that hardware, but closer to the time of the purchase they become aware that it has a fundamental incompatibility issue with the rest of the school's system. Rather than see this as time wasted, they have learned something more about what the considerations are, while at the same they have created a plan, much of which will still be useful. It's key to focus on the positives at times like this, as a way of sustaining momentum.

These six mechanisms will help the team make meaningful progress. From this it's then important to routinely celebrate and reward success and achievement. Encourage teams to keep a record of their achievements so they are not overlooked in the drive to get to the next milestone. Offer recognition for the achievements of the team in staff meetings. If it's possible to offer small rewards like taking the team out for dinner, or giving them a half day off, for big milestones reached, then do that, but recognition does not have to involve a financial cost. Often a sincere "Thank you" and clear recognition for the work is enough.

⚙ Task 2.2: An effective team

Think back to a successful and effective work team you were involved in and reflect on the following questions:

1. How do you know it was effective?
2. Can you identify the things that made it a success?
3. Were the things mentioned in the six mechanisms above in place?
4. What can that experience tell you about effective teamwork?

Getting started

Having created the team (or allowed the team to self-organise), the team's first three priorities are:

1. to create a set of clear objectives (with the understanding that these may evolve as the project does)

2. to use these objectives as the foundation for communicating the message to all

3. to begin critically evaluating the technology options that meet the need

The first of these priorities must be done first, but, depending on context, the order of the second and third priorities might be reversed.

Objectives

The team begins their substantive work with the very important task of taking the goal we created in the previous chapter and turning it into a clear set of objectives and sub-objectives. (Sub-objectives are the smaller goals or steps you need to take to achieve your main objective. These can't be defined until a clear main objective is established, and breaking the goals down into smaller objectives may help keep you on track, as well as make success seem more achievable.)

⚷ SMART and SMARTER objectives

Using SMART and SMARTER objectives is a way for us to ensure that our objectives are focussed and powerful in guiding use toward a specific end-point. They are applicable in many settings, both work-related and personal, and when it comes to managing change in our institutions, can be extremely important in the process.

SMART stands for:

- **Specific** (What precisely is it that the team is setting out to do?) Make sure your objective uses language that all stakeholders can understand and helps them identify the context and project as easily as possible.

- **Measurable** (How will the team know whether they have achieved it?) All objectives need to be measured or quantified. While this may not necessarily be in numbers, progress and achievement of the goal needs to be identifiable and stakeholders need to be able to determine if they are making progress toward completion, or have indeed completed the project.

- **Agreed** (Is the team clear and united on these objectives?) As part of your role leading the project team, you need to work toward full support from all team members. Ensuring they completely understand their role, the overall objectives and the long- and short-term impacts of the project, can help you gain their buy-in and commitment to the project and objectives.

- **Realistic** (Is this feasible?) While this may seem simple, often the nuances of change can mislead people into thinking something may be more simple, or more complex, than it is in reality.
- **Timebound** (Is there a deadline?) This should be a simple but powerful inclusion in your objectives, to ensure everyone is aware of the timeline you are working with and keeps it top-of-mind as they work.

SMARTER adds two extra points to consider:

- **Engaging** (Is the proposed solution attractive to end users?) As you think about the needs of your stakeholders, you should keep in mind the elements that make the solution appeal to your end users as well as to the committee working to put the solution in place.
- **Relevant** (Does the solution fit with the current and evolving LTO culture and the ways in which you work with your learners?) Making sure that the proposed solution fits with your organisation and its needs is extremely important in achieving success. Including this information as you specify your objectives and sub-objectives is important to the programme's success.

The added *ER* of 'engaging' and 'relevant' are important and apply most directly to the solution you are proposing – clearly the addition of this technology to your programme must be relevant to the way things are done, and, furthermore, if it is engaging, it is much more likely to inspire even those people who are reluctant to connect to new technology.

Objectives make it clear exactly what you wish to achieve, and unlike the goal, which can be used to 'sell' the change and communicate clearly what you want to achieve, the objectives take that overall endpoint and make it concrete. It answers questions such as, "What exactly is to be done, by whom, and by when? And what is the extent of the change?"

One aspect of developing the objective (or objectives) will be to make a list of all the features and functionality that you would like the new software, for example, to have. At this stage when looking at technological change, you may not actually know all the things you are looking for, because in many cases we are not in a position to really know what is possible or what exactly can be done. It will likely be better to look at something which meets all the needs you think you have, yet is flexible and potentially extendable.

An example of such an objective and sub-objectives might be:

Goal: to add a blended component to our upper intermediate courses

Overall objective: to launch the new course with blended supplementation – materials online, teachers trained in their use, students given clear guidelines and support in the platform and materials – by the beginning of the next semester

Sub-objectives:

- to consult with the level teachers to identify areas of the syllabus which could be moved into a guided self-study area, by the end of week 2
- to train up to four volunteer teachers (materials team) to convert or write materials for the platform, by the end of week 4
- to have the materials team develop content for the supplemental course, by the end of week 10
- to hold a workshop for all teachers to ensure all can use the platform, investigate new materials, and give feedback, during week 11
- to prepare a student training session, to be given in week 1 of new courses
- to launch the new blended course in week 1 of Semester 2, and to monitor and provide support (to teachers and students) throughout the semester

Q Case study: A well-resourced team working with objectives

A university language programme in Sydney, Australia, created a specific department (Technology Enhanced Teaching and Learning, or TELT) for the introduction of new technology in its teaching programmes. However, early results were not great.

The first initiative, in 2009, involved the installation of interactive whiteboards (IWBs) in every classroom. This was a costly exercise that had a polarising effect on teaching staff across the organisation. Despite several training sessions and the best efforts of in-company mavens, the uptake was quite limited. Many teachers were reluctant about, or even averse to, using them. Some departments left it up to the teachers to determine their use, which was often minimal. Some teachers largely ignored the IWBs, bemoaning the loss of half their previous whiteboard space. Terms such as "dumb-boards" and "white (board) elephants" were frequently used across the organisation to describe the units in many classrooms.

On reflection, the IWBs failed to live up to their proclaimed potential for the following reasons:

- They were perceived as having only symbolic benefit.
- They were a 'fad' that management responded too quickly to (a common problem, according to Fullan (2001a)).

- Departments failed to create short-term wins.
- The organisation failed to create a sufficiently powerful guiding coalition (as suggested by Kotter, 1996).

With the lifecycle of the IWBs coming to an end, and the need for the university to expand and create over 50 new classrooms due to a surge in student enrolments, the university re-entered the market to find a more suitable replacement model. While the adoption of IWBs in 2009 was a move initiated and championed by management, the need to change to a new model was largely driven by negative teacher feedback about their experience of the IWBs. Most teachers saw attempts to integrate the IWBs into curricula as having little "relative advantage" (in the words of Rogers (2003)) and being a burden to their workloads.

Early in 2015, a committee of teachers was formed, along with two representatives from the TELT department, to choose a more suitable replacement. Within this committee, the TELT representatives played the role of 'champions of change', while the teachers were made up of a mixture of the various characters in Rogers' (2003) **Diffusion of Innovations curve** (see panel below). Initial meetings were dedicated to establishing a teachers' wish list of functions for the technology that would replace the IWBs – with no assumption that this would actually need to be IWBs; essentially they were deciding on the next generation of classroom AV equipment.

Over the course of four months, the committee grew to include several in-company IT personnel, as well as the deputy CEO. Their purpose was to assist the education departments' transition to more suitable AV classroom equipment as quickly and smoothly as possible. Finance was a secondary consideration to agreeing on a model that suited the needs of the teaching departments. Different groups of stakeholders were surveyed and eventually a wish list of features, effectively a set of objectives, was created. In summary:

- One particular group of teachers wanted data projection, touchscreen capabilities and the continued use of Smart software (as many of their lessons now used this software);
- A second group of teachers were interested in data projection but little else. Their main desire was to have more write-on whiteboard space;
- Both groups wanted a simpler, more flexible model that was less prone to glitches.

In order to meet the divergent needs, the IT committee members conducted market research and provided the committee with a number of options. Once the teachers narrowed the options to a shortlist, they visited a display centre to spend an afternoon testing the models, eventually settling on an Interactive Data Projection (IDP) model that projected data onto a non-reflective 'write-on' whiteboard. It was something of a compromise between the needs of the different groups of teachers mentioned above, but it satisfied the primary needs of teachers across the departments. Coupled with a more effective training and support mechanism than had been present with the IWBs, the change was much more successful. Within a year of introduction, a cross-campus survey discovered that uptake was very nearly 100%, and the IDP introduction had quickly become 'business as usual'.

⚷ The Diffusion of Innovations curve

In 1962, E.M. Rogers proposed a model of how quickly different people adopt innovations. He suggested that technological innovations were eventually taken on by everyone in society at different speeds, depending on their psychological profile. 'Innovators' and 'early adopters' are very quick to adopt the innovation, while 'laggards' tend to be the last to adopt the technology.

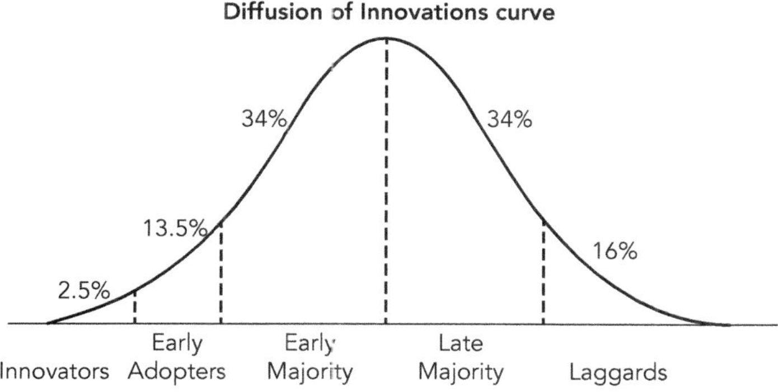

Figure 2.2: Rogers' Diffusion of Innovations curve (Rogers, 2003)

Communicating the objectives

Once the team has begun its work, and specific objectives have been set by the teams working on the change, it is time to consider how to communicate the change and decisions to all the various stakeholders who are less involved in the change process. This begins with proper messaging, which will help keep stakeholders informed about the progress of the change implementation and also avoid panic and misunderstanding, as well as maintain a positive approach to the change.

In fact, clear communication needs to be happening at all points through the process of transition, here at the beginning, then all through the process. Communication ensures that people do not feel in the dark about what is happening, that unfounded rumours do not spread, and that people remain engaged and enthused about the coming change. Also, it tends to mean that people who are in any way challenged by the change will feel able to say so and ask for assistance.

One important element of managing change within an LTO of any kind is ensuring that the messaging is appropriate and will support a positive change. This is one of the first and most important tasks that must be tackled by the team working toward change. There are a few issues to think about when working on the messaging around the change, which can be broken down as follows:

1. Timing. It is essential when dealing with any transition in the organisation that the messaging around that change begins *before* the change is apparent. It is generally advisable that there be some sort of formal or semi-formal announcement made which ensures all students, faculty and staff receive one unified, true message around the change. Rumours and misinformation can be very damaging and cause people undue stress and worry, and it's best to preempt that as a possibility. Also, it is important to involve stakeholders in a timely manner which allows them to ask questions, express their concerns or excitement, and also prepare both mentally and logistically for the change.

2. Focus and word choice. Focus on a positive message. Often, messages going out within teaching organisations mention or lead with the reason behind the change, which, while not wrong, can start the message off on a negative. Even if the change is being promoted to correct or fix something within the organisation or within the teaching/learning process, a stronger focus is to lead with the idea of improving what is already happening. Use strong words and conviction in your message: instead of saying, "we hope this new element will lead to improvements in learning", say, "we are certain this new element will lead to improvements in learning". Reference the added value of the solution you are implementing and craft the message in a way that is comfortable for your organisation. Often, LTOs use words that are familiar and specific to their context and stakeholders, such as saying something like, "we know that the East High School Otters will benefit from this new programme". Crafting your message in this way keeps it personal, focussed and positive, which helps to obtain stakeholder buy-in.

3. Delivery mode. It is often best to communicate more than is perhaps actually needed when it comes to big changes, but even smaller changes or those with less impact need to be communicated widely. As instructors and administrators at LTOs, we often hear how students and faculty rarely pay attention to emails, or don't seem to log in to shared platforms as often as desired. Leaders often find themselves repeating information or resending emails. When change will impact, find ways to ensure the message is received in various mediums. Virtual posters or flyers in the computer lab, announcements on the message boards, parent bulletins, class announcements and meetings are only some ways of getting the message out there. What are other ways that might work for your population?

4. Follow-up and reinforcement. While this may seem simple, ensuring that all your members have the same, unified message is very important. Nothing is more frustrating or damaging than when people receive different or even conflicting information about a change. Remember that all change, even when positive, is difficult, and it's important that the whole institution have the same approach. Commiserating with an angry student, or agreeing that the change isn't the best, will undermine its potential success. As much as possible, try and get everyone on board with sharing a unified message, and ensure they get the support they need to see the benefits of the change (see the section on dealing with resistance in Chapter 3, for more on this). While this may be easier said than done, when promoting a change, it's nearly impossible to make everyone happy. Undoubtedly, there will be some left disappointed or in disagreement with the decision. Make sure their voices are heard and an open forum is available for them, even as the project moves forward, and remind them this is the appropriate forum to express their disagreement, and not in the communication they may have with other stakeholders and end users.

(See **Appendix 3**, **Appendix 4** and **Appendix 8** for more advice on planning how you communicate with the project team.)

Stage 4: Selecting

Once the team is formed, and there is a set of clear and specific objectives on which the team is focussed, it is important to have a methodology for making decisions around the technological solution which will be chosen and implemented. While technology continues to change, the need for new technological solutions will not disappear within the institution, so enabling the team to make decisions around technology is important. However, it can be tricky, especially considering the sheer number of technological solutions available. In order to make the best choice, it is important to approach technology with a framework for making decisions and working toward implementation.

Tools to evaluate technological solutions

Although several models exist to help users implement new technology into classrooms (e.g. SAMR and TPACK – both of which will be explained in this book), there are not many to help users evaluate the different options available to them and decide on a solution (Brush and Saye, 2009). In fact, the literature points to few tools for managers – and mostly to ones based on educational technology and not designed necessarily to take into account other types of technological integration which may in fact be more relevant to the learning situation.

When it comes to the learning outcomes for the integration of technology, one model, **The Triple E Framework** (see Figure 2.3), is designed to help teachers choose technology based on an understanding of how students learn (Kolb, 2017). This model has emerged as a strong tool for evaluation of technology, and even provides suggestions on how students may engage with the technology in their learning most effectively in the form of instructional strategies, but does not necessarily address the administrative- and organisational-culture questions behind the implementation and choice which managers must be ready to address. Thus, this framework, while a tool that can be used to evaluate at the academic level, is limited for LTO managers in its scope for supporting decision-making.

While nations, states and governing bodies provide guidelines about what technology should be used for, they do not offer much support for choosing the technology to use or integrating this technology into the institution. Additionally, there is little available focussed on language institutions and their specific needs in a way that can help guide managers through this process. This is probably because there are so many different kinds of technology available and so many different teaching situations. Therefore, rather than providing a list of specific questions to ask when evaluating technology, we will suggest a model that can help you develop your own questions – the SELECT model.

🔑 The Triple E Framework

The Triple E Framework (Kolb, 2017) was designed to support primarily K-12 teachers bridge their understanding between research and implementation while choosing technology for their classrooms. It's a tool for educators to easily evaluate how to select tools to meet their learning goals, and to design learning experiences using technology that have a positive impact on student achievement and learning outcomes. The framework is meant to be used to support teachers in their instructional choices around and with technology. While it is focussed on the integration of technology and how to choose those tools which will contribute to positive learning outcomes, it does not provide a holistic framework taking into account the stakeholder needs outside the classroom.

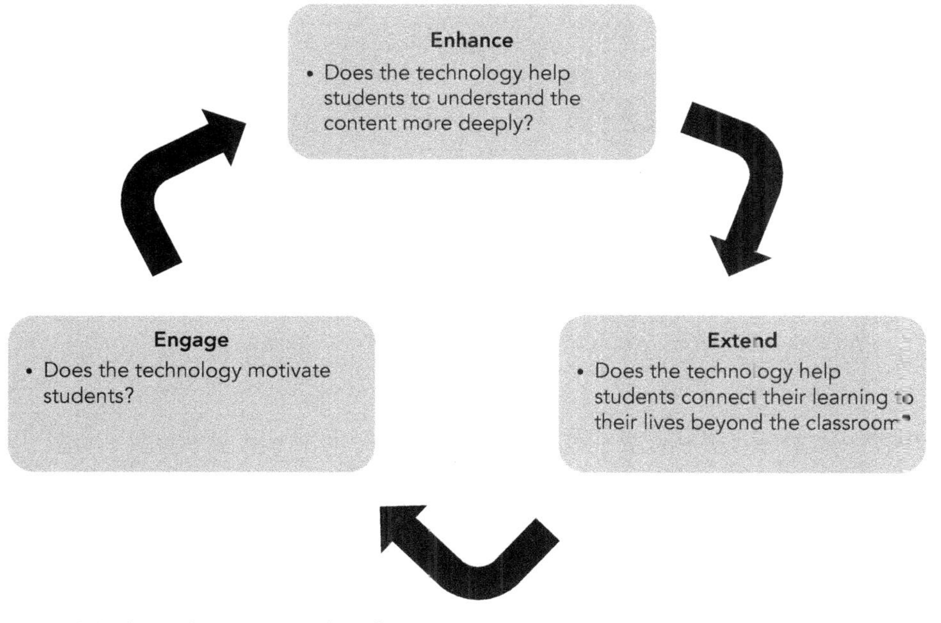

Figure 2.3: The Triple E Framework (Kolb, 2017)

The SELECT model

The model we propose provides a simple, holistic, structured way of analyzing options and transmitting decisions in a way that will hopefully satisfy the various stakeholders. The intention is to give managers a concrete, clear and concise way to address the elements which need to be considered when choosing technologies for the learning environments. It is a process that takes into account logistical and administrative considerations, as well as the limitations and expectations of both cost and stakeholder need.

This SELECT model proposes the following stages:

- Set objectives
- Explain and expand
- List contextualised criteria
- Explore options
- Cross-examine
- Take forward

These stages can help managers not only evaluate the technology, but also build a proper case for promoting this change within the institution and with all stakeholders. We will describe the methodology in detail, following the flowchart below (Figure 2.4).

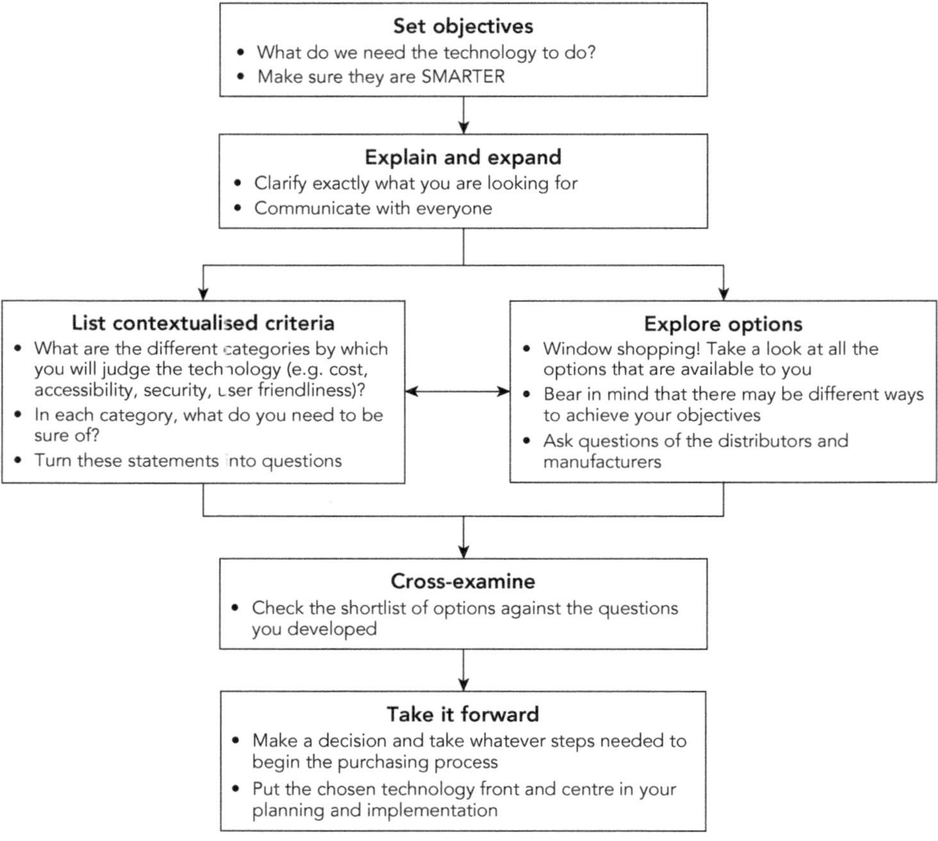

Figure 2.4: The SELECT model

1. Set objectives

The first stage of this model was covered in the previous section, so you have already articulated the goal and developed a set of concrete objectives. Ensure that the whole team is familiar with these objectives (as they relate to the choice of technology itself). If the objectives do not clearly lay out what you are searching for, here is the opportunity to add objectives to the list that do. These objectives will inform the rest of the process that follows, so it is crucial that they are clear, unambiguous, and mutually understood by the whole team.

2. Explain and expand

The next stage of our model is to take these objectives and ensure that we are very clear, to everyone, about what we are looking to achieve and, just as importantly, what we must be sure to avoid. This is all about communication – communicating the objectives you have come up with to the various stakeholder groups, as well as what exactly they mean, and also communicating within the core team to be absolutely certain that everyone is in agreement as regards the choices to be made.

A good starting point is being clear about why we are making the change. In order to be able to communicate this effectively, it is important that managers and teachers understand exactly why and how technology should be used in the classroom. If the use of technology does not add value to the teaching/learning process or provide some sort of advance in administration of the institution, then it is likely just technology for technology's sake, or a bad implementation of what could potentially be good technology, and managers may want to reconsider the reasons behind considering its use at all for this particular need.

In some cases, schools set usage goals or standards surrounding how much technology should be used in the teaching. For example, there might be a percentage goal could be set of how much content per course should be available online or as self-access using some technology, or even what percentage of courses should be blended (partly online, partly classroom-based) rather than given in a traditional face-to-face setting. With growing concern over integrating more online in general, but also in these specific cases, it is increasingly important that institutions and their stakeholders evaluate the value that the technology may add. This is to avoid following a technology trend or overusing 'edutainment'.

☌ The Gartner Hype Cycle

A visual representation of the dangers of being influenced by fads, or of a belief that technology will solve problems instantaneously, is provided by the Gartner Hype Cycle, which tracks the adoption and phase of maturity of technologies in the marketplace and can help users be more realistic about the effectiveness of the technology, and how long it will take to effectively integrate, as well as get a sense of the way that the market works (see Blosch and Fenn, 2018). The Hype Cycle places technology solutions on a curve that balances the public hype around the product versus the usability and effectiveness or capability over time. Around since 1995, this is considered a reliable model in the technology field and one worth exploring as you look at technology solutions.

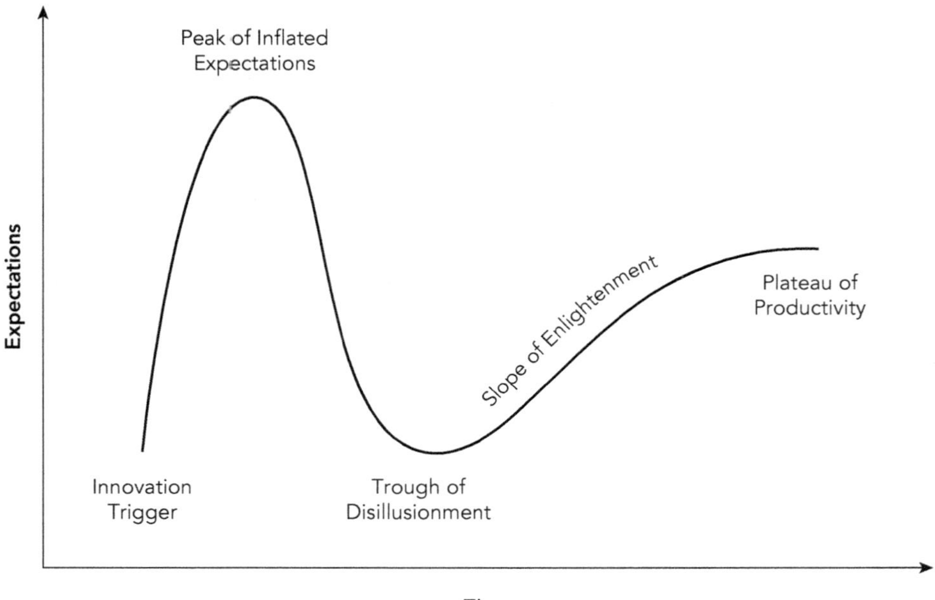

Figure 2.5: Gartner Hype Cycle

In brief, the cycle depicted here describes the following trajectory of many innovations. In the *Innovation Trigger*, a new technology or new way of doing things emerges. There may be initial professional or media interest at this point, which really takes off in the *Peak of Inflated Expectations*, in which initial publicity is very positive, because some presentations at international ELT conferences or good marketing help, for example. Some schools may quickly jump on the bandwagon, while others adopt a wait-and-see policy. At this stage the cycle enters the *Trough of Disillusionment*, when the promised benefits of the innovation seem to be far lower than the initial hype suggested. At this point, perhaps the innovation disappears altogether. Eventually, we reach the *Slope of Enlightenment*, in which teachers, for example, begin to work out ways of making the best use of the technology and perhaps do surprising and unexpected things that hadn't been imagined or foreseen by the manufacturers. New examples of how the technology can benefit students or classroom practices appear and are spread via social media or conference presentations. Perhaps the innovation is developed further, and add-ons created. Finally, in any successful new technological product, hardware or software, we come to the *Plateau of Productivity* and the technology becomes part of the mainstream, is seen as very common and useful in most of the profession, and is widely found in many contexts, perhaps used slightly differently.

It's possible to see similar reactions when a new piece of technology is introduced into an LTO – initial excitement can quickly be followed by disillusionment, before the technology is slowly taken up and becomes normalised. Training, which will be addressed in Chapter 4, is key here, as it can help to flatten this curve and avoid people having expectations that are too high.

Understanding what the technology will bring to the process is an important issue in defining the problem and goal, and in getting stakeholders in agreement with its use and integration. We believe that decisions around educational technology integration should stem from the critical academic impact it may have: how it can contribute to the teaching-learning process, what value it will add in student learning and outcomes, and how it can enhance and/or facilitate the learning process, as well as how it might affect the motivation and productivity of students and staff using it. While some teachers and managers are very good at making effective academic decisions surrounding change in programmes, content and curriculum, technology can often add in an extra, complicated element. For this reason, it's important to have a tool that can help managers and change leaders analyse the different options while also keeping in mind the different considerations each tool may provide, including cost, time and stakeholder buy-in, among others.

3. List contextualised criteria

The first two stages of the SELECT model are designed to ensure that there is a high level of clarity across the team, so that the objectives are extremely clear. Having done this, it is time to get down to the details. In this case, this involves taking the objectives and turning them into a list of criteria against which any technology options can be judged. This model is partially based upon the approach that Brian Tomlinson (2013) recommends for materials evaluation (such as choosing a new coursebook), but it is a very good starting point for us in this process too, and we have adapted it accordingly.

The initial phase of this is simply to have the team list any and all criteria for the evaluation of the technology that spring to mind. This forms the 'idea pool' which will act as a starting point to develop your criteria. Then, take the various criteria from the brainstorming session and try to categorise them in some logical way. This has two benefits – firstly, it allows you to organise things for the later stages so the process is more logical and helpful, and secondly, the act of categorisation may spark ideas for other criteria in the various categories.

To give an example of how this might work, imagine you are looking at selecting a new VLE for an additional online component to your face-to-face courses. Perhaps your objectives include "Create an online component to intermediate classes for adults on a VLE". The brainstorming may come up with a list of criteria that includes things such as: easy for teachers to create and upload materials; secure; can be accessed by students with low bandwidth; can be accessed on a mobile phone; within a certain budget, etc. These may be categorised under the headings of 'teacher usability', 'security', 'student accessibility', and 'cost'. (Note that this is just a quick example – many more categories are likely to be brainstormed too.)

You should find that you have two types of criteria: some things that are either true in the case of a particular solution or not (e.g. can be accessed on a mobile phone) and some that call for an evaluative judgement (e.g. easy for teachers to create and upload materials). Separate your criteria out into these two types.

The first type, things that are either true or not, can be turned into yes/no questions (e.g., "Can the content be accessed on all mobile phones?"). When looking for potential solutions, you should think about these questions first to narrow down the list of solutions. After that, you can use the second list of criteria to evaluate a limited number of solutions in more detail.

It will aid this evaluation if the second type of criteria are turned into questions which will be easy for the reviewers to answer (whether the reviewers are core team members or others who are invited to take part in the evaluations). In order to allow for comparison between similar solutions, you should use open questions that require reviewers to assign a numerical score (e.g. from 0 to 5). This will allow you to total the scores for each potential solution at the end and use these scores to guide the final decision. As you write these questions, check that each one only asks a single question, that it is answerable, that it is (as much as possible) objective, and that it is not open to interpretation. If some criteria are more important than others, they should be weighted to reflect this. Table 2.1 lists some example questions for the online component situation described above:

Table 2.1: Example evaluation grid using questions

Criteria	Score (0 = not possible, 5 = great)					
	0	1	2	3	4	5
Teacher usability						
How easy is it for teachers to create and upload materials?						
How flexible is the grading tool?						
Security						
How easy is it for the IT department to lock the system down in case of a breach?						
To what extent can students and teachers be given unique and secure log-in information?						
Student accessibility						
How user friendly and visually appealing is the mobile version?						
If a password is forgotten, how simple is it for the student to recover access?						

An alternative approach is to use statements and ask reviewers to agree or disagree with them, as shown in Table 2.2 below:

Table 2.2: Example evaluation grid using statements

Criteria	Score (–2 = strongly disagree, 2 = strongly agree)				
	–2	–1	0	1	2
Teacher usability					
It is easy for teachers to create and upload materials.					
The grading tool is flexible.					

One of the things that you should do at this stage is to ensure that the choice you will eventually make is fully contextualised. One of the biggest flaws in decision-making surrounding technology is that the evaluation of potential solutions does not take into account important issues relating to the specific context in which the technology will be used. For example, managers need to ask how this integration may fit with budget, space and equipment, beyond the short term into mid- and long-term considerations, and training and usage questions, as well as questions around partnership and prestige. Creating a list of evaluation criteria with these issues in mind ensures that important considerations are not forgotten when assessing the options.

To prompt you to consider some common context-specific issues, **Appendix 5** provides some suggested questions that you could use as part of your evaluation. This is not an exhaustive list (because every context is different), but it should help you to see the kinds of issues that you need to be thinking about. Another useful tool can be found at Workforce EdTech (https://workforceedtech.org/tool-evaluation-criteria/). This provides some critical questions to consider and even an evaluation rubric that can be used to guide you through these questions.

Finally, trial the questions – ask some of the team to use the questions/checklist to evaluate the technology you are looking at. If all the team were involved in building the list, ask some potential end users not in the team to go through them and see if they are clear, and if they could easily answer them in as objective a way as possible.

We will take a look in slightly more detail here at two specific and extremely important areas – cost and educational technology integration – that should be considered when developing your list of criteria.

Cost

Clearly, while the primary driver of change and of moving towards a new way of doing things using technology must be what the innovation *adds* to the way of doing things, it is impossible to ignore the question of cost. The act of change itself costs money and is "resource hungry" (Fullan, 2001b), while, of course, new technology always comes at a price.

It is important that the team which is making these decisions is aware of the budget that there is for the purchases they will need to suggest. In addition, it would also be worth helping them understand all the factors that go into decisions of this nature. Remember that the team should be representative of different stakeholders. It is a great risk to assume these stakeholders understand each other's focus or interests, or that they all understand the financial tensions involved in the successful running and improvement of the LTO. A short training session can be given on the concepts of cost, price and breakeven, which will help them to be aware of things such as: opportunity costs (closing a classroom to open a technologically equipped self-access centre means you have one fewer income-generating classroom); disruption (rewiring classrooms inevitably will mean some disruption and often classes being forced to relocate for some time); training (purchasing new software and licences is not the end of the costing as staff will require training); and maintenance (costs do not finish after installation), as well as financial benefits to the innovation such as increased student numbers, marketing advantages, streamlined processes taking less time, and so on. A checklist for this process is included in **Appendix 6**.

Educational technology integration

One other area that is perhaps less tangible, but no less important, is how smoothly the technology can and will integrate into the educational programme. Various models have been created to assist people in evaluating whether a piece of technology will suit their educational needs. One of the most well-known models is the **SAMR model** (see panel below). It should be noted that the model is specifically related to educational technology (as opposed to school management software, for example).

When using the SAMR model to aid evaluation (as opposed to integration), the team could be encouraged to think about what stages in the SAMR progression the new technology needs to support. For example, if the solution is very limited, it may only allow for use at the level of substitution. However, more sophisticated solutions may allow initial use for substitution or augmentation, and then, as time goes on and the technology becomes more integrated in the overall programme, it could open up new ideas and possibilities. When developing criteria, the team should be thinking about whether expanding the use of the technology in the future is important for the solution or not.

4. Explore Options

In this stage, the project team should explore the various technology options which could potentially meet the needs identified above, using the list of yes/no questions developed above to narrow them down to the final most important 'fit for purpose' solutions. This allows the team to disqualify some solutions as options for further exploration and confirm that others are viable options for the programme.

⊙╼ SAMR Model

The SAMR (Substitution Augmentation Modification Redefinition) model is perhaps the best-known model in the language teaching context. It describes four levels of technology integration – going from 'substitution' (the least sophisticated) up to 'redefinition' (the most sophisticated). It encourages teachers to think about the different ways that technology can be integrated into the classroom.

For example, consider the way that the SAMR model can apply to a simple classroom writing task of composing a persuasive essay on a given topic. Step one, substitution (S), could be when that task is completed using word processing software (as opposed to paper and pen). Augmentation (A) here is when students use the other functions of the word processing software (such as the spell check or the thesaurus) to improve and develop their writing. To modify (M) the task, the teacher may ask the students to cooperate on their writing, using collaborative writing tools such as Google Docs, working together to edit one another and develop their writing jointly. Finally, the task becomes redefined (R) with the addition of multimedia elements into the writing, and perhaps their publication on a blog to share with the world.

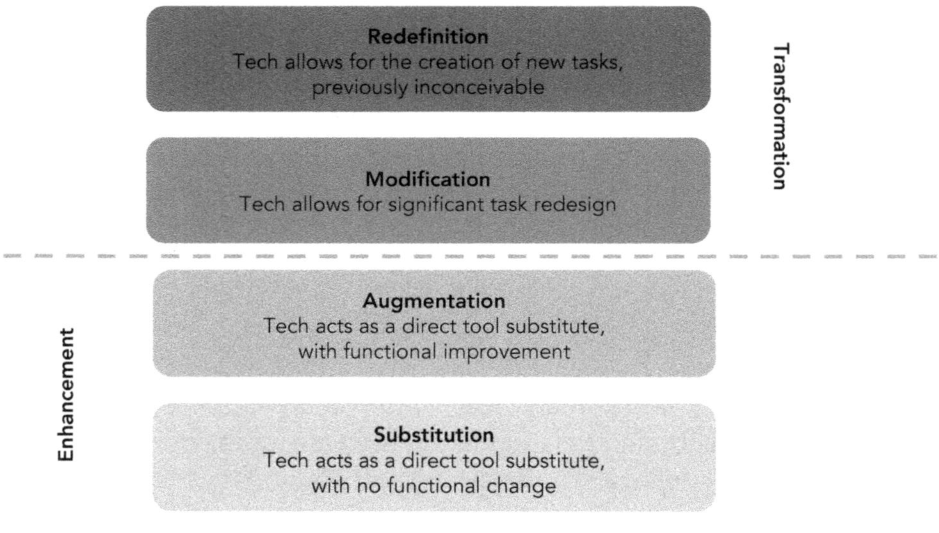

Figure 2.6: The SAMR model (Puentedura, 2009)

Exploring options will involve research into the various possibilities available that may exist. The search should not be limited by the kind of technology you think you need – focus on your objectives and examine different options. For example, if the LTO needs to have some way of providing a platform in which students can interact with one another and the teacher, and complete tasks outside the classroom, then it is likely that the research will involve looking into the various VLEs that are available on the market (and possibly building one from scratch); but other options which are not specifically designed for this kind of interaction could also be considered, such as a combination of messaging and document sharing software. To give another example, if the need identified was for technology to support and supplement teaching in the classroom, then the research could include projectors, interactive whiteboards, tablets for students, and possibly other solutions too.

Although it's important to consider a range of options, it's equally important to narrow down these options to a manageable amount before conducting a more in-depth evaluation. While most language school managers are not specialists in technology, more often than not they will play a central role in discovering the products or services available to solve the problem or identify the correct solution. Often, language learning-focussed companies, as well as technology companies, approach potential clients to sell technologies that may add value to the institutions. Parents and teachers and other stakeholders bring in their own experiences and biases, and the ideas and offers may seem overwhelming as well as enticing. As managers are not usually involved in the world of technology, figuring out which solutions to even consider can seem like a daunting chore, and one that takes dedication and a clear focus on outcomes.

There are a couple of starting points that can help with this initial narrowing down of possible solutions, which may be worth taking into consideration as you get started with the evaluation process.

First, it's important to always remember your main objective. Don't let any excitement and glamour around a product distract you from this objective. It's valuable to file away ideas and options that might suit future situations at your LTO, but a good deal or an exciting technology should not distract you from the main objective.

Second, don't underestimate the power of your community of practice, your professional network and your contacts who are working with technology or perhaps encountering the same issues to solve at their institution. Hearing their experiences or filtering your ideas with these professional contacts may be the most powerful feedback you can get, if you can count on their honest, critical opinions.

5. Cross-examine

We now have a list of products to investigate and a list of evaluative criteria to use to assess the options. Have each member of the project team (and perhaps others whose thoughts might be helpful in providing a more rounded picture;

even students might be involved) evaluate the different choices separately and then collate the results, ideally in a meeting, so that the core project team members are fully involved.

Once you have identified a small number of promising options, piloting products and services (especially in large institutions) can give you an opportunity to try out the product or service without the same financial commitment as a full implementation may imply, and allows you to collect feedback and data around use. This can help you to not only evaluate the effectiveness of the possible solution, but also to gather invaluable feedback from users as well as other stakeholders. Each test situation, with well-collated feedback, will allow you to build a strong case and analysis of each option, which can be used by the team to make final decisions. Piloting, of course, should happen after your initial filtering of solutions; you won't want to pilot several options, but only one or two of the most viable you have identified.

6. Take it forward

Once the different solutions have been evaluated using the questions, you will, hopefully, have built up a clear idea of which technological solution is the best option for the programme. Hopefully the final decision will be made unanimously by the project team, or at the very least with a clear majority. If not, it may be that the project leader will have to make the final decision. You will also have developed some fairly objective criteria to use for evaluation, which will help put you in a much better position to explain to the various stakeholders why you have made the particular choice – something which is of great value when talking to those who may be required to authorise the financial outlay, as well as the various staff members who may need to be convinced of the usefulness and appropriateness of the option chosen.

Summary

In this chapter we have discussed how teaming is an essential element of making a strong coalition, not only for decision-making, but also for selection and future implementation. We have also looked at how communicating the issues is critical to success, and how making and keeping clear objectives is central to the process.

We have also proposed the SELECT model for selecting the technology to use. This involved creating a list of criteria, filtering initial options, and then evaluating a set of solutions before making a final decision.

📖 If you want to find out more…

Amabile, T., and Kramer, S. (2011). *The progress principle: Using small wins to invoke joy, engagement, and creativity at work.* Harvard Business Review Press.

This is a very well-researched guide to how managers can foster progress and enhance the work life of their employees. The book doesn't just look at effective teamwork, but at effective management in general, with lots of examples and real cases.

Edmondson, A. C. (2012). *Teaming: How organizations learn, innovate, and compete in the knowledge economy.* Jossey - Bass.

Amy Edmondson, Novartis Professor of Leadership and Management at Harvard Business School, makes a case for the role of teams in the modern organisation. Based on years of research, this book shows how leaders can make organisational learning happen by building teams that learn.

Gladwell, M. (2000). *The tipping point: How little things can make a big difference.* Little, Brown.

This book is an enjoyable read about the way that change can come about through a certain moment when the idea behind the change suddenly takes off. The book looks at ways that ideas can be disseminated and promoted.

Tomlinson, B. (Ed.) (2013). *Developing Materials for Language Teaching* (2nd Edition). Bloomsbury.

This is a very useful primer on materials development in ELT in general, with chapters written by a number of well-known experts. It also includes Tomlinson's own key chapter on materials evaluation.

3 Planning the change

- explains the importance of clear planning in the implementation of your change
- identifies strategies for dealing with risk – both in terms of mitigation and contingency planning
- shows how to analyse stakeholder groups and their various needs – and how to communicate with them
- looks at the various reasons why people might resist change and develop strategies for dealing with each
- explores ways of integrating technology into your programmes

Introduction

In the previous chapter, we proposed a model (SELECT, Figure 2.4) to help you in deciding the technology you will use. We also discussed teaming as essential for decision-making and implementation, and communication as central to the success of your project. In this chapter, we will discuss the importance of stakeholder communication and project planning, as well as expand on the evaluation of technological tools.

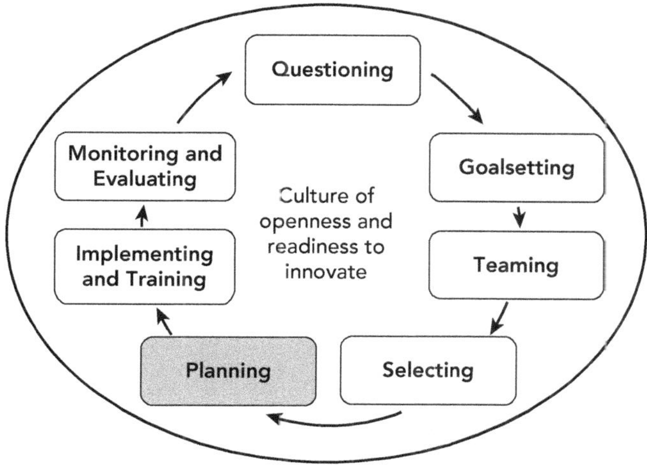

Figure 3.1: The stages of technological change

Stage 5: Planning

It is vitally important to plan the change well, and to think through all of the things that may come up. As with any plan, it is important to be flexible too, but ensuring that there is a clear set of tasks and activities that are well thought out in advance is essential. The case study below illustrates how change can go wrong when planning is less than thorough.

Q Case study: A poorly planned change

In a large private university, after over eight years using the same content, methodology and approach to teaching in the English language programme, university leadership pressured the Language Centre to find ways to make the programme more efficient in terms of time and finances. The management team made the decision to move to a blended learning model of English language teaching, reducing class hours from five face-to-face hours per week to three per week during the 15-week cycle. The content and materials were updated to support the new approach, which required students to complete online self-study activities outside of class to support the in-class learning, using a flipped classroom approach.

The Programme Director spent several months working with her team, with university leadership, and with their content provider to prepare for the change in the programme. Great care was taken to ensure that all the campus-based Language Coordinators were aware of and trained in the programme, and many hours were spent creating a set of standardised lesson plans to guide teachers and students in this new way of teaching and learning. The budget allotted to the programme was extremely limited, and though leadership had endorsed the change in theory, very little support from central academic offices was received by the language team during the process. This lack of presence caused friction within the language team both centrally and on campuses, and affected how the messaging of the programme was shared and received at the central and campus levels. There was scepticism surrounding the change, but the team forged ahead and requested feedback in the hope of establishing constructive ways to avoid issues during implementation.

The language team had many years of experience and was especially careful to ensure that student registration, grade transfer and payment, as well as course assignments, were as smooth as possible. At the same time, many hours were invested in training for the Coordinators, who would be piloting the programme during the first semester. The hope was that onboarding (initial administrative training, platform training, and pedagogical introduction to the programme approach) with Coordinators would help cascade training down to teachers in the future. As launch date approached, the team was excited and had taken great pains to cover all their bases. At the same time, the university leadership seemed to be nervous and began to demand more and more reporting and feedback on the new programme.

The day arrived, and the feedback coming from campus was not positive. The teams seemed to have trouble getting students set up with the online components of the course, even though campus Coordinators had been instructed on how to work with the new programme and share the information. Students didn't seem to be enrolled correctly in the classes, and the Coordinators couldn't understand how to begin the programme on the platform, despite many hours of training. Students began to complain and other departments within campus allowed students to register for different traditional courses instead of the new programme. University leadership began to question the programme and demanded more accountability and reporting. The Programme Director started to feel overwhelmed and frustrated and felt neither herself nor her team were being listened to by the rest of the stakeholders. Ultimatums were made by the Academic Deans, tensions were high, and the programme seemed to be at risk. The content provider, despite a commitment to support the programme, seemed to pull back to let leadership sort the issues, and the core team was left with a very complex situation to sort out.

In this chapter we will use a **project design** approach (see panel below) to go through the phases of implementation and planning. The case study presented above is just one example that, even as you plan, there is a constant need for review within the process and a deep understanding of, and commitment from, the stakeholders that represent the complex layers of organisation involved in the change. Even with the best planning, teams leading change should be prepared for possible problems to arise along the way. These elements of the process are much more specific and targeted than the work we have done so far. To use a metaphor, in previous chapters we have drawn up a vision for our new house and laid the foundations. Now it is time to start building the structure.

Implementation of programmes begins with planning, a fundamental activity which will directly influence not only the ease with which programme change can be accepted and implemented, but also how success can be understood during the process, in the short, mid and long term. It's also important to note here that while we are concerned at this stage about planning and implementation, communication should not be forgotten and overlooked. Keeping all the key stakeholders informed all the way through the process is a crucial way of ensuring buy-in, and also of ensuring that any doubts or obstacles that we may have missed are raised as soon as possible.

⚷ Project design

Project design is a rational, logical, sequential process which answers four key questions:

- Where do we want to go?
- Where are we now?
- How do we get from where we are now to where we want to be?
- What will we see along the way (and at the end)?

In order to effectively answer these four questions, a number of tools are employed to build up a clear plan, some of which we have already seen and a number of others of which are in the next chapter.

Where do we want to go? This question is about identifying the need and the goal. It may involve creating a set of SMART(ER) objectives (see Chapter 2). It also means thinking through the outputs and outcomes of the proposed project (see 'Outputs and Outcomes', page 77).

Where are we now? Answering this question means thinking about the resources we have, and the constraints and obstacles we might face in reaching our goal. This might involve using a SWOT analysis (see Chapter 1), as well as a risk assessment and a stakeholder analysis (see Tables 3.3–3.5 below).

How do we get from where we are now to where we want to be? This is about generating and choosing the best strategy, which will be a set of activities and tasks to be performed, as well as creating a clear timeline of when these tasks will be carried out. The structure of the project will be defined here, as well as the budget, personnel, and action plan.

What will we see along the way? To answer this question, you need a monitoring and evaluation plan for the project (see Chapter 4).

For most technology implementation projects, the simple linear approach described here will be appropriate. However, for projects that involve the development of new content or new technology, an **Agile** approach can also be useful. This approach to project management began in software development, where new features were gradually added and tested (often to a live project). For most change processes of the type described in this book (essentially one-off investments), this iterative approach is probably not the recommended one. It is not in the scope of this book to look in depth at agile project management; however, if you wish to, a good place to start is: www.atlassian.com/agile/project-management

Tasks and scheduling

After the core team has come up with a set of objectives and has selected the technological solution that they think best meets the needs of the organisation or department, the next stage is to use these objectives to develop a series of clear steps – tasks that need to be achieved in order to get to the identified objectives. Each objective, or sub-objective, involves a number of tasks that need to be completed in order to reach that point. The team should brainstorm all the things that need to be done (without worrying about the order in which these tasks should be done). Once these tasks have been listed, then they can be ordered and each one assigned to someone. It is very important that each task has someone associated with it. Even if this is not the person who actually carries out the task, they will be the one responsible for ensuring that it gets done and reporting on its progress. You should also assign a deadline to each task and make notes as to which tasks are dependent on other tasks: does one task need to be completed before the next can begin, or can they proceed in parallel?

Once you have ordered and connected up these tasks, deciding which are dependent on one another, they can be entered on a **Gantt chart**, which allows you to do a number of things: have a clear idea of when certain resources and people will be needed, make sure you have the financial and other resources in place, note when there are key milestones in the project, and monitor the project to see how well it is progressing. Figure 3.2 shows an example Gantt chart for a project to make level tests computer-based.

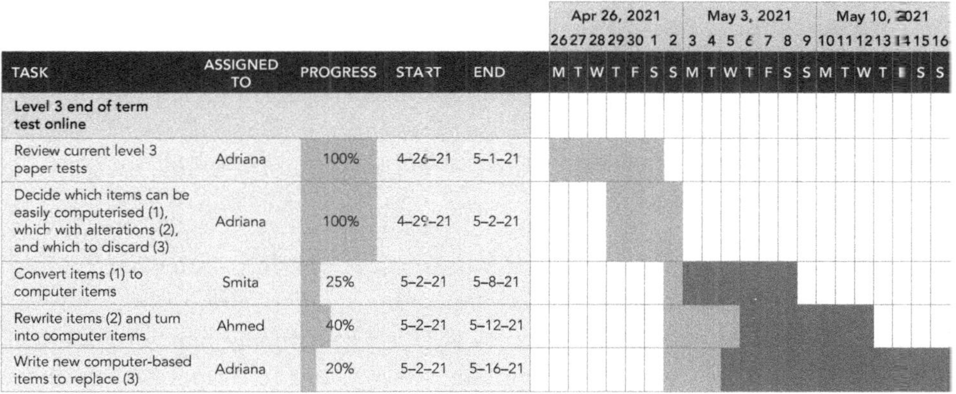

Figure 3.2: Sample Gantt chart (using a template from Vertex42.com)

Using a simple free template such as the one above (or other project management software), you can reasonably easily create one of these charts, which enables you to keep track of the project and refer to it whenever somebody asks about the progress of the work. It's also possible to share the chart with others, so they have access to the latest information too. In the context of a team-led process, having an overall plan like this to refer to is invaluable in keeping the momentum going and making sure everyone is on track. We will cover the monitoring and evaluation of the project in depth in Chapter 4, but this kind of Gantt chart is an extremely important monitoring tool.

(See **Appendix 7** for some project planning guidelines.)

Risk assessment

A key element to thinking through any project of this type is to be aware of the various risks and obstacles that the project may come up against. Of course, it is entirely possible to simply respond to problems as and when they arise, but a clear risk assessment plan with actions to be taken will not only save time, but in many cases will ensure that you successfully avoid the problems occurring in the first place.

The types of risks that these kinds of projects are likely to face include:

- opposition from leadership
- financial problems (e.g. costs too high, budget overspend)
- technological compatibility (e.g. new software does not integrate well with currently used software)
- having to make do with something that only partially addresses the need
- technology breakdown
- resistance from key people

The last of these is perhaps the most common, and we will look at this area later in the chapter.

You may not be able to think of or plan for every possible issue that could come up, but you should be able to identify many of the potential problems. Going through the assessment process at this phase in the planning allows you to work on the various risks and devise strategies to, hopefully, ensure that the problems do not materialise.

For each risk that the team identifies, decide how likely it is to occur and how much of an impact it would have if it did. Having done this, think through both **mitigation strategies** (which are designed to stop the risk occurring) and **contingency plans** (plans that are put in place in case, despite your best efforts, the risk comes to pass).

Table 3.1 below provides a basic example of this approach, for two of the risks that you might identify in the computer-based test example mentioned previously:

Table 3.1: Example of risk assessment

Risk	Likelihood	Impact	Mitigation strategies	Contingency plans
Students find it difficult to use the test-taking interface in the software.	Medium	High	Develop a set of practice exercises and mock test items for in-class practice before the test date, and ensure that teachers use them and devote class time to familiarising learners with the interface.	Ensure that invigilators are watchful for problems and trained in the software so that they can quickly help. Invigilators should also be empowered to make decisions regarding allowing students extra time to complete items if necessary.
Hardware or software crashes during the test.	Low	High	Rigorously test the software on the machines that will be used.	Train invigilators in different possible responses, up to and including reboot. Empower invigilators to make decisions on allowing more time or giving students another chance to take the test.

Task 3.1: Thinking about mitigation strategies and contingency plans

Using the framework described above, think through the risks associated with a project you have led or collaborated on in your LTO. Reflecting on a past project may help you more clearly identify the concepts before attempting the exercise for an upcoming project. Think of how risk and mitigation strategies might have been (or perhaps were) implemented in this project.

Now, think about an upcoming project and make notes in a grid like the one below to map three potential risks, mitigation strategies and the contingency plans you can put into place to prevent negative impact.

Table 3.2: Risk assessment grid

Risk	Likelihood	Impact	Mitigation strategies	Contingency plans

Stakeholder analysis

Much of the risk we are likely to encounter is actually connected to project stakeholders. These may be the end users of the software we're introducing, those who control the budgets, or any of the other interested parties. Each stakeholder or group of stakeholders has their own needs to be met or specific interests in the project. As each is looking to fulfil those specific needs, it is crucial to understand the different needs and wishes of each stakeholder group and be ready to act accordingly and proactively to lower potential risk. We'll look at how to conduct a full stakeholder analysis below, but before that it's important to introduce another important issue which originates within our stakeholder groups: **resistance**. In any change management process, dealing with resistance is a key area of the work.

Resistance

There are a number of reasons why people resist change, and as a manager hoping to create change, it is important to be aware of them. Only by understanding the reasons why people resist change can the manager hope to clearly communicate the vision, addressing their fears and concerns. Below is a long, but non-exhaustive, list of some of these reasons, along with some ideas for strategies to deal with that kind of resistance. This list is drawn from experience and from discussions with other academic managers. As you can see, there are a number of reasons why change can be a tricky process to manage – even in the case when the need for change seems clear to everyone.

1. Purpose of change not made clear

People need to know why the change is happening. Is it because there is research that shows the advantage of it? Is it because the students are asking for it? Is it because it will make things work in a more streamlined way?

Strategy: Make sure people can see clear reasons for the change. Keeping track of all your stakeholders' needs (perceived and real) can allow you to effectively and continually communicate with them as you move through the process. As we've discussed in other chapters, this element of communication is ongoing, and stakeholders need to be given the information personalised for their interests, and stated in language that speaks to them.

2. People affected feel change reflects badly on their past performance

In some instances, people can worry that the need for change is directly related to something they or their department has done poorly or in some way failed at. This may, in many cases, be entirely illogical, but it is clearly a barrier. If the change *feels like* it has been forced upon the organisation as a result of poor performance from those who need to be deeply involved in the change, the result may be a less than positive attitude towards the change.

Strategy: Reassure them. As in (1) above, make clear the reason why the change is happening. Involving your stakeholders in the process also allows them to question and add their own input, thus giving them a forum in which this type of insecurity can be quickly clarified and their buy-in can be strengthened by their involvement.

3. Key job characteristics are changed

If the change seems to be changing staff job descriptions in a fundamental way, this will create resistance. Even if additional responsibilities are linked to additional compensation, the change of one's job is, on some level, a change of identity, and not something that people can handle with total ease. A teacher being asked to add a blended component to their classes may perceive things in this way, for example.

Strategy: You will need to present this in a way that values and recognises the central component of the employee's job, while also outlining the benefits to their professional growth and development. A teacher, for example, may need to be reassured that the proposed change does not in any way change the centrality of teaching in their work, and that rather it adds a level of knowledge and skills to what they can do. Ensuring you have open lines of communication around this also allows for teachers (or other stakeholders) to maintain a level of autonomy and input into how the change is implemented and may contribute to less resistance in the long run.

4. People affected by the change not involved in planning change

This is key and a reason that is often overlooked. Management-imposed change that impacts primarily on the classroom, for example, is likely to be resisted by teachers and consequently by students. The end users of the new technology must be deeply involved in the planning of the change, as mentioned previously. If the steps already listed in this book have been followed, this problem will be largely avoided, but there still may be those who feel like they were overlooked.

Strategy: Ask those who are involved and key members of the core team to keep in contact with their colleagues and peers, outlining and explaining the details of the project and inviting feedback and concerns so they can be addressed.

5. Fear of the unknown

Sometimes people can feel a lack of certainty: "What is this going to look like?" They may doubt or distrust that the new technology will actually improve upon the status quo.

Strategy: Here is where your vision we developed in Chapter 1 comes into play. You will need to paint a picture of the future, describing what the end point of the change will look like and the benefits that it will bring to everyone.

6. People connected to the old way

Many people will be familiar and happy with the old way of doing things, even if they can see that it is imperfect. Teachers, for example, may have built up a bank of materials, resources, tricks and workarounds with the system they have been using. Giving up on the old way means a lot more than simply changing some aspect of the technology. Even something as seemingly simple as a change of coursebook can cause some teachers to feel that they are losing out on the specific activities and exercises they have perfected as part of their work with the old coursebook.

Strategy: As in (4) above, get feedback from people – either directly or through their peers in the core project team. As the change comes into being, ask staff to be on the lookout for positive things they feel are being 'lost' and respond accordingly – for example, by asking people to find ways to mirror that beloved feature in the new system. But also make sure they look for the 'bright spots' in the new system and build on them, rather than just looking for the problems.

7. Belief that it's a fad

Any teacher who has been around for a few years will have seen innovations that have turned out to be fads. This may mean they invested a lot of time and effort in these innovations, which ultimately felt wasted. Such missteps are inevitable – we never get it entirely right, especially where technology is concerned and where research and development is proceeding at high speed. There will always be times when something is introduced and then becomes obsolete or simply unfashionable very quickly. Even new technology that was a success can be superseded quite rapidly. Because of this fact, it can be hard to convince people that what is being planned is something that is worth them investing time in.

Strategy: It will be important to convince them of the sustainability of the innovation, and potential ways it will be developed or built upon in the future. Having a plan which shows how the change will be adapted and evaluated can help show stakeholders that there is indeed a strong model (such as the one in this book) supporting this new integration, and that this is not a hastily implemented change without a real foundation for success.

8. Fear of failure

The individual in question might have concerns about being 'found out' or otherwise not being successful in handling the new change (or the new job – see (3) above). This may particularly be true of a few teachers who tend to be in the 'late majority' or 'laggards' categories in Rogers' Diffusion of Innovations curve (2003) (see Chapter 2), and who perceive some of their colleagues as being far more enthusiastic and able in the realm of new technology.

Strategy: Make it clear that no one will be left behind and that training and support will be available at all times. Ensure that everyone feels able to express any worries or doubts they have to at least one person on the core team.

9. Lack of confidence in people's capacity to implement the change

We've all heard stories of large organisations or government departments which have installed a new software system that has been badly implemented, gone hugely over budget, or proven not to have been thought through as well as it should have been. Even if we are confident in our ability to deal with something new, we might have doubts about others – whether it be the programme administration, outside suppliers, or even our colleagues. The thought process (consciously or unconsciously) goes: "If enough people can't make the new system work, perhaps it will be shelved – and if that happens, it will be better for me if I haven't invested a huge amount of energy in preparing for the change."

Strategy: Focus communication on the achievability of the change, and highlight and celebrate the milestones in the Gantt chart you prepared, so that everyone can see progress is occurring on schedule.

10. Belief that it's for the benefit of someone else

If a teacher suspects that the introduction of a classroom innovation is not actually directed at the teachers or learners, but rather at some other stakeholder (for example, to save money for the institution), they may well hold back on their involvement.

Strategy: If the change has been driven by the key stakeholders, as suggested in this book to this point, then this one should be avoided, but it is still important to stress the benefits of the change to those whose jobs will be most affected.

11. Lack of support from key people

It's possible that those dealing with the change may move forward and devote their energies to making sure that things work well, but be frustrated or restrained by a lack of support.

Strategy: It's important to ensure that everyone gets the support they need (such as training or mentoring, for example), but also that everyone in the core team is aware of who they need to be ready to support and what kind of support they might need to give (and where to go to find that support if they cannot offer it).

12. Details of the change are poorly communicated

In some cases, the need for the change and the vision for the change have been well articulated, but the details are unclear to people. This comes back to the difference we noted in Chapter 1 between *change* and *transition*. People need to know what steps they need to take, when they can expect certain elements of the change, and what they will need to do.

Strategy: Focus on the details as well as the big picture. What will happen when? What do we expect to happen? What milestones are there? What will show us that change is happening? All of these questions you have thought about already – there is no reason to keep this information from people.

13. Change introduced too quickly or too slowly

Some changes need a lot of preparation and the foundations need to be in place before the implementation of the new technology can take place. If this is hurried or not planned effectively, the change will feel rushed and this can provoke resistance. On the other hand, occasionally the process of change is overdone and takes much longer than is necessary and people become distracted or bored.

Strategy: In setting your goals and objectives, be realistic about the length of time needed to implement a change, but also don't make it take too long. Communicate deadlines and milestones (so that people know when they will see progress, and be able to see those milestones when they occur).

14. Exhaustion/Saturation

While change is a constant and we must always be alert and aware of the need for change, from time to time change can become too much of a constant. Human beings need some stability and they need time to turn a new situation into 'business as usual'. In a situation in which change seems to be piled on top of change, people can become overwhelmed and saturated with change.

Strategy: Pay attention to the collective mood of your team. If they have just successfully completed a major change, don't instantly start the next one. Congratulate them, reward them, and give them a break.

Task 3.2: Reflecting on resistance

Think back to a change that you were involved in as a recipient, rather than as a change agent.

1. Did you resist the change in any way, or did you respond positively from the beginning?

2. If the former, why and in what ways did you resist? If the latter, what was it about the change and the way that it was introduced that inspired you to be enthusiastic and engaged?

Now think back to a change that you managed.

1. Did everyone respond positively?

2. If there were people who resisted, why do you think they did? Go back to the 14 reasons above and identify the ones which possibly were behind the resistance.

How can we articipate and plan for resistance?

As mentioned earlier, a stakeholder analysis is a good way to think about the needs of the different stakeholders and any potential risks connected to them – including the potential for resistance – as well as the actions you could take to mitigate these risks. One way to conduct this analysis is with a stakeholder analysis grid. Here are two examples, using a format suggested by the Project Agency (n.d.).

In these examples, the LTO has decided to introduce a VLE to supplement face-to-face classes with online materials and exercises. Tables 3.3 and 3.4 show we could analyse two groups of stakeholders, teachers and students, with regards to this change:

Table 3.3: Example stakeholder analysis for teachers

Stakeholder	Their interest in and requirement from the change	What the change needs from them	Perceived attitude or risks	Action to take
Teachers	An understanding of the value of the new system to their students' learning Training in using the VLE Support in creating materials/ exercises C arity on their responsibilities	Buy-in Involvement in decision-making Creating materials and exercises Their encourage-ment to students in becoming active and making use of the system	Fear of being asked to do more work for no more money Worry that students won't access the VLE or gain from it Enthusi-asm (for some) Doubt and fear (for some)	Invite teachers to be involved in the decision to choose the VLE and structure of any materials creation templates Once chosen, create training modules (in house?) Use early adopters and mavens (Glad-well, 2000) to start creating banks of materials

Table 3.4: Example stakeholder analysis for students

Stakeholder	Their interest in and requirement from the change	What the change needs from them	Perceived attitude or risks	Action to take
Students	Better learning outcomes (and belief that the new system will contribute to that) More motivating 'homework' tasks Ease of access on any device at any time	Buy-in Honest feedback on the VLE and its use Completing online homework in the system Active participation in using the system	Frustration of having to integrate a new tool and fear of it being boring Enthusiasm (for some) Intimidation and fear of making mistakes (for some) If it feels like 'homework', possible lack of engagement, or simply ignoring it	Invite students to give feedback on the use of the VLE and include their suggestions in future reviews of content Create student walkthrough sessions to ensure easy access and use of the VLE Identify student 'champions' of the use of the VLE and invite them to encourage other students

Of course, this kind of stakeholder analysis grid can be used to think about all the different stakeholder groups, including those who wield power. By this stage in the process, you already have agreement about implementing the change from those who control the budget (assuming that this is not you). However, if a project needs significant financial outlay, then the person in charge of the budget will want to be kept updated and informed of the progress of the work. They will notice significant delays and want to know the cause of these delays, or at the very least they will require regular updates. Clearly, most stakeholders will want to be informed about how things are progressing, but for the 'funders' (even if they are internal, they are still, arguably, the project funders), this is absolutely crucial – not least because they have the power to cancel the project entirely. Using the same template for the project mentioned above, but for senior management, might look something like this:

Table 3.5: Example stakeholder analysis for senior management

Stakeholder	Their interest in and requirement from the change	What the change needs from them	Perceived attitude or risks	Action to take
Senior management	Efficient, cost-effective change process, that leads to an improvement in the work of the organisation, and potentially enhanced reputation and attendant marketing/ financial benefits	Continued support Potentially, advocacy and lobbying within the wider organisation Sometimes, active involvement and interest to highlight the value of the change to others	Initially enthusiastic and have been convinced (and hence have approved the change) Will be worried if the project takes too long or starts getting out of control	Keep them updated Submit regular reports If there are delays or potential problems coming up, make sure they are informed If other people in different departments /areas need to be brought on board, ensure that the leaders support you

(A decision tree for communicating with stakeholders can be found in **Appendix 9**.)

Outputs and outcomes

Any project generates both **outputs** and **outcomes**. *Outputs* (occasionally referred to as 'deliverables') are the concrete things produced as a result of the project – the purchase of new hardware, rewiring of classrooms, teacher training sessions, materials put in the cloud, and so on. *Outcomes* (also known as 'impacts') are much less concrete but are the hoped-for effects of the change – such as more streamlined processes, better student performance, efficiencies in coursework delivery, happier students, and even higher student numbers.

With all project work, there is a danger that we allow the outputs to distract us from the outcomes. This is because we can see and measure the outputs and they serve to demonstrate to senior management and stakeholder groups that we are getting on with things and producing visible effects. We can report that 100% of the teachers have attended the three training sessions that we created, and it is a statistic that sounds impressive. What's harder to say is whether those teachers learned anything or whether they have used the skills provided in the training in their own teaching – and it's even harder to see whether the students have benefitted.

For this reason, it's worth the team trying to find ways of expressing the outcomes that are hoped for as a result of the change. This will ensure that those outcomes are kept in mind and continue to inform the focus of the change process. It will also mean that reports to senior management not only outline which of the promised outputs have been met, but also how the effects of the change are being observed. It also means that the team needs to devise methods of evaluating these outcomes, so that the effectiveness of the innovation can be seen. (More on evaluation can be found in Chapter 4.)

To give an example, let's refer back to our example project from earlier in this chapter, of introducing computer-based level tests. This project has the objectives of greatly reducing teacher time spent performing certain simple tasks involved with the testing process, and reducing paper usage, while having no negative impact on assessment outcomes.

So the outcomes for this project might be:

- The percentage of students being placed in the correct level in the next semester remains at the current number (or improves)
- The amount of time taken by teachers and other staff in administering tests in tests is reduced to 10% of current levels
- Consumption of paper in the testing system is reduced to zero

 Task 3.3: Outputs and outcomes

Think of a change you are planning to make or could make in the future, or think about a change you already went through.

1. For this change, what are the outputs and the outcomes?

2. If the outputs are clearly marked on your Gantt chart or other project plan, how can you ensure that you are keeping your hoped-for outcomes in mind? Could you post them somewhere where you and others can be constantly reminded of them, for example?

Implementing the change, and being aware of the J-Curve

When planning a change, it's easy to think that you just need to plot a course from your current state (where you are now) to your desired state (where you want to be), and the journey between the two will be one of gradual improvement – like the dashed line in Figure 3.3. However, no matter how well planned out and thought through this transition is, it will nearly always cause disruption. In reality, change looks more like the dotted line in Figure 3.3. This is known as "the J-Curve" (Viney, 2005) because of its shape. Rather than a rapid and easy transition from the current state to the desired state, in fact there will be a large dip in performance, caused by the disruption to standard processes.

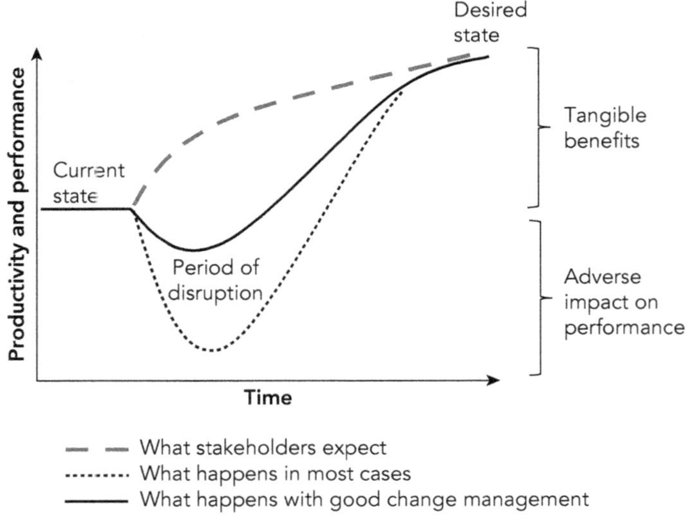

Figure 3.3: The J-Curve (Viney, 2005)

However, with good change management processes, including good communication, training and support, we can get to the middle line in Figure 3.3. This illustrates how good change leadership and management can minimise (though not entirely overcome) the disruption.

While you will notice a distinct difference in the depth of the curve between the line that represents the reality of most situations and the line that shows the effect of good project management, it is important to note and accept that change, even in the best of cases, will require a period of adaptation, and it would be unrealistic to expect no resistance or disruption in the process. As leaders, the best we can do is to embrace the nature of change and plan for it accordingly in our process. If we are not able to accept negative feedback and are unprepared to deal with any resistance, then it is likely worth readjusting our expectations as leaders. As explained above in the discussion of resistance by stakeholders, this part of the process can be difficult, but it in no way reflects negatively on the performance of the leaders working toward the change. It is also important to make the various stakeholder groups aware of the typical J-Curve pattern – nobody benefits from having unreasonable expectations that will not be met.

As a leader working through the process of change in technology, you have by now built up the tools you need to deal with and support your stakeholders in dealing with this effectively. First and foremost, you know your academic programme and its requirements, and you have acquired knowledge and experience of the selected technology which you can use to respond to the concerns of the rest of the team. Don't be afraid to confront the harsher realities of change head-on. Let your work and the work of your team take the lead in guiding people through the stages of resistance, and reassure them that you are in this together and that your process allows for their feedback and opinions.

The implementation of educational technology

The process described above is for the implementation of a change project in general, but it is important to look at what the implementation of educational technology specifically looks like. In general, we could say that effective integration of technology results in a situation in which the use of the technology is routine and part of business as usual. In the specific case of *educational* technology, the innovation clearly supports curricular goals.

As well as being an evaluative tool in the SELECT model, the SAMR model (introduced in Chapter 2) also offers a clear structure through which educational technology can be integrated into the curriculum. Its clear step-by-step approach highlights the process through which educational technology moves from being something new to something that is totally integrated with our work. This is a useful reminder both to consider the different possibilities of technology and to gradually implement its use in stages – rather than trying to do everything at once.

Following the model, the technology starts to be used, at first, as a **substitute** for things that teachers previously had been doing. To give an example, with the abrupt shift to online teaching made necessary for many programmes by the Covid-19 pandemic, the online classroom initially became a direct replacement for the face-to-face classroom, with teachers trying as much as possible to replicate the way they would work with students in the physical classroom.

The next step is **augmentation**, where teachers use the technology to add to their teaching, rather than simply replacing like for like. In the example above, perhaps teachers and students were able to use their smart phones to augment the way that these new online lessons were working – using messaging functionality to converse in pairs while still in the online classroom, to simulate the different types of written production students might experience between formal and informal writing, say.

Modification, the third step, means the teaching-learning process is substantially altered with the support of the technology. The lessons and planned learning outcomes are changed as a result of what can be achieved with the technology. Using our above example of the current changes due to Covid-19, the teacher uses online discussion forums to increase the amount of writing included in the programme, which in turn allows them to increase the scope of the learning objectives achieved during each level.

Finally, with certain technologies, we reach the fourth step, **redefinition**, in which the task as a whole is redefined, and the technology supports a whole new approach to reaching the learning outcomes. Again, in the example from before, the teacher sees the usefulness in the changed circumstances in promoting a more flipped approach to learning, allowing students to learn new material at their own pace in an asynchronous way, while using the synchronous online classroom to promote discussion and mutual support.

It is important to note, however, that the SAMR model does not necessarily imply that every new technology must reach the 'R' stage. The model is a continuum and while the implementation of some technologies by some teachers will possibly get to 'R', others will simply be used as convenient substitutes for more traditional methods (the 'S' stage).

🔑 The Technology Integration Matrix

As part of the focus of the integration of technology tools for learning (as opposed to admin or assessment technology), we would like to draw your attention to the Technology Integration Matrix (Florida Center for Instructional Technology, 2019). In this model, there is a five-stage process of technology integration, briefly outlined below. In addition to the technology integration process presented below, the Technology Integration Matrix looks at incorporating characteristics of meaningful learning at the different stages.

1. **Entry**

   Here the teacher begins to use the new tool in their lesson, supplementing or augmenting their previous teaching with the technology.

2. **Adoption**

   Now the teacher shows the students how to use the tools, giving them training in the basics of their use, so that they know how to operate them.

3. **Adaptation**

   In this stage, the students begin using the tools independently, and the teacher's role is to facilitate and support them in their exploration of possibilities.

4. **Infusion**

   The teacher now simply provides the task and its outcome, and the students make choices about what technology to use and in what way in order to reach the desired outcome.

5. **Transformation**

   The teacher encourages the students to use technology in an innovative way that leads them to higher order thinking.

   This is another useful reminder to implement the technology in stages, allowing users to become comfortable with a limited use of the technology before moving on to more complicated tasks.

🔑 The TPACK model

Another well-known framework for evaluating the integration of technology is the TPACK model (Roddy et al., 2017) – Technological Pedagogical and Content Knowledge. This model was built with the foundational idea that teaching is an organic process and that success in teaching is born not only from content knowledge, but also from understanding and working with the unique circumstances of each learning environment, learners and expected outcomes, as well as how teachers interact with the actual content which is to be taught.

The model outlines the idea that good teaching with technology comes from the three core components of the model, 'technology', 'pedagogy' and 'content', and the interaction among and between them.

Content refers to the content knowledge that teachers must have (and courses must contain, by extension) in order to ensure students receive correct information and training around the content itself. Each academic discipline has its own set of related knowledge and skill sets that must be learned, and it is critical that teachers have proficient content knowledge and are able to relay that knowledge to students in an effective manner.

Pedagogy in this case refers to the teachers' deep knowledge of the teaching methodologies and frameworks associated with the content being taught. This is the teachers' practice in making content accessible and understandable for students, and understanding and transmitting the nuances of the learning focus in each field of study.

One of the strengths of the TPACK model is that the model recognises the fluid and constantly evolving nature of **Technology**. The model requires that users recognise this fluid state and understand the role of technology deeply enough to know that its application must be based on the way it can support learning, and not on the individual characteristics of the technology itself, which may become obsolete even before it is fully integrated.

Understanding that the decisions made around content can impact the type of technology that can be used, and that, conversely, decisions around the type of technology to be implemented can also impact the way in which we interact with and transmit content, is an important element in the function of the model. This understanding around the way that content and technology can influence, constrain and even exploit one another is an important element the model addresses, and becomes perhaps even more important when we consider that the integration of technology includes (ever increasingly) the integration of technologies *not* designed specifically for educational circumstances.

🧠 Task 3.4: The integration of technology

Think back to a successful example of technology being integrated into your programme. How did you know it was successful?

1. Think about the **content** that was considered when integrating the technology. What about this content made the use of technology important or relevant? Why was there an interest in technology being part of this content? What value did the integration add to the content knowledge teachers were working with?

2. What were the **pedagogical** elements of the programme that made the integration of technology successful? How was the methodology adapted and influenced by the use of the integrated technology? How did the technology add to or improve the pedagogy with which teachers were teaching in this particular content and programme?

3. When the **technology** was evaluated, which elements of the chosen technology were those that made this the correct integration for the programme? How did the technology change the way the content was taught and received by students? How did the technology improve the learning experience and contribute to the success of the teaching and/or class administration?

Thinking about this example, how could the TPACK model inform future evaluations of technology in your programme? How do you think this model might strengthen the programme and what elements might need to be explored?

Clearly, there is the need to implement the technology and the change itself in the sense of a management task, but there is also the need to integrate the technology as an educational tool into the wider working of the programme itself. To a large extent, once the technology is purchased and installed, and people begin working with it, the way that this integration proceeds is determined by the users themselves, teachers and students, for example, in the case of in-class software. This integration may happen in stages, or it may happen instantly; it will depend on the technology, its use, and to some extent the context and the staff in the place where you work. It's important that you and the core team are aware of this and have a sense of how the technology is hoped to become part of your curriculum, as well as other possible ways that it might happen. Once the technology is 'part of the furniture', so to speak, the effects on the curriculum, assessment, training and all the other aspects of academic management will grow from the use itself.

In the following chapter, we will look at the training and support that will need to go into this integration, as well as the systems to put into place to evaluate the effectiveness of the change and the hoped-for enhanced educational outcomes

Summary

In this chapter we have explained the key considerations of planning in implementing change, which can guide the planning and ultimately implementation of the desired change. This will involve developing a clear plan of action, with the change broken down into tasks that are assigned to specific people with deadlines. We also looked at strategies to overcome resistance and making contingency plans to respond to possible problems.

In addition, we have discussed the positive implementation of new technologies into your programmes, and thought about how the technology may be integrated into the educational work you do, bearing in mind various factors and various approaches. We can now move forward in the next chapter to the final stages of the model for technological change, which will address the continual evaluation and feedback we need to focus on as technology and our programmes evolve.

 If you want to find out more...

Everard K. B., Morris, G., and Wilson, I. (2004). *Effective School Management* (4th Edition). Paul Chapman Publishing.

> This is a wel -known and well-regarded text on school management and leadership, specifically directed at helping teachers with senior management responsibilities, and the schools and colleges that they work in, to become more effective.

Florida Center for Instructional Technology. (2019). *The Technology Integration Matrix.* https://fcit.usf.edu/matrix/matrix/

> A useful matrix, designed to aid technology integration in education. The matrix links five characteristics of learning environments with five levels of technology integration to provide a comprehensive model.

McKenzie, K., Misel, K., Parkerson, L., and Sconzo, T. (2017). Consider the human element before racing your next initiative to the finish line. *The Jabian Journal.* https://journal.jabian.com/consider-the-human-element-before-racing-your-next-initiative-to-the-finish-line/

> This article outlines the importance and value of using change management strategies, specifically those which deal with supporting and responding to people (human capital management), when managing projects.

White, R., Hockley, A., van der Horst Jansen, J., and Laughner, M. (2008). *From teacher to manager: Managing language teaching organizations.* Cambridge University Press.

> For a long t me the only book on ELT management, and an industry standard. It includes two chapters especially important for us in this context, on change management and project management.

4 Monitoring and sustaining change

This chapter:

- reviews the final two stages in our technological change cycle: Implementing and Training, and Monitoring and Evaluating
- considers ways to ensure that adequate, relevant and necessary training and professional development is provided
- highlights the value of consistent and inclusive monitoring and evaluation
- reflects on the evaluation of success with a view to further/wider application
- explains how certain tools can help set up programmes for long-term success

Introduction

Returning to our change cycle (Figure 4.1), we will be focussing in this chapter on the final two sections of it. We will look at the implementation of the project plan, in particular, how training can be carried out in a way which ensures that everyone is successfully served by it. Furthermore, we will discuss monitoring and evaluation – the ways that this can be carried out successfully and, importantly, the uses to which the evaluations can be put, both in terms of the ongoing change process itself, and of extending it – within and outside the organisation. Finally, we'll wrap up the cycle by looking at ways in which the whole process can be reflected upon and lessons learned.

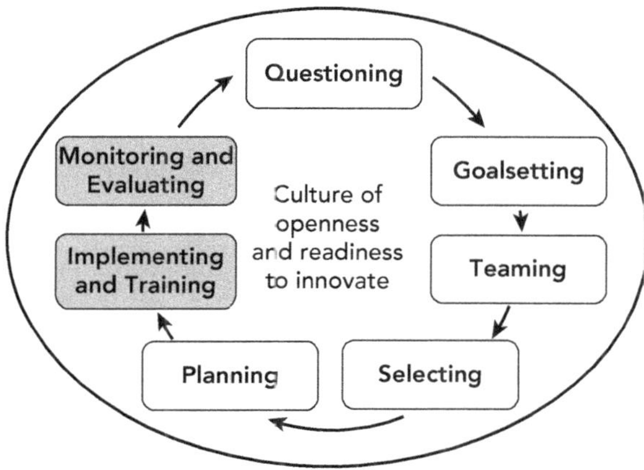

Figure 4.1: The stages of technological change

Stage 6: Implementing and training

A common mistake with training

Training people in the effective use of a technological innovation has to be looked at from three angles:

1. The features and functionality of the technology – what it can (and can't) do.
2. The needs and approaches of the users themselves.
3. Ways of combining (1) and (2) to effectively incorporate the technology in the user's work.

Unfortunately, training in technology often starts and ends with the first of these. A representative of the technology company visits and explains the functionality by giving a "do this, then do this, then click here" demonstration. Teachers may initially feel well served by this kind of training, because foundational knowledge of function and use are important to begin successfully using a new tool. However, much of this information is likely to be forgotten later, and although manuals and video tutorials may supplement the instruction, most people find them an unhelpful way of acquiring the relevant skills.

Additionally, if the training stops here (which it often does, due to time, budget and other restrictions), teachers and students may not be able to properly harness the power of the technology and tools being implemented. Because teachers rarely ask how the technology serves to meet their needs, they begin to adapt their teaching to fit the technology itself, which is the wrong approach. The same key questions need to be asked during training as should be asked when assessing and choosing new technology: What are the real needs that should be addressed and how can this technology work to facilitate that? Training, therefore, needs to be an **inclusive** and **hands-on** process.

The intersection of functionality and needs

A better approach is to focus on the intersection of what the technology can do and what you want the technology to do – the area marked 'Convergence' in Figure 4.2 below. Obviously, the hope is that the convergence represents a much larger area than this and instead is a very significant overlap. However large it is though, the representative from the technology or publishing company will want to demonstrate all the features and functionality (including the part to the left of the diagram), whereas your goal must be to try and focus on the convergence and also on expanding the features to the right (as per the arrows here).

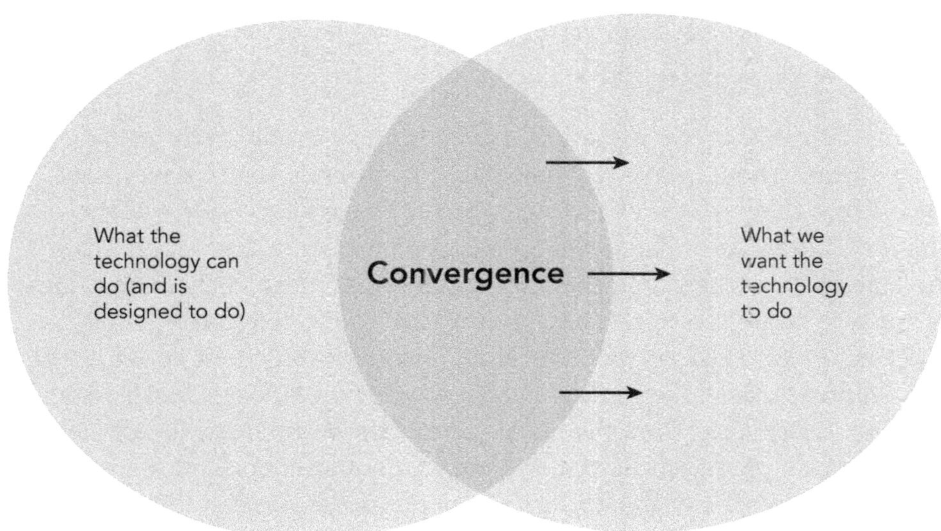

Figure 4.2: The intersection of functionality and needs

If you are lucky enough to be able to work with the technology provider to develop and improve their product – rather than simply buying something off the shelf – then you may be able to ask for more features to allow you to do more of the things you need to do. This can be a mutually beneficial relationship, as you get the features you need and they get a better product to sell to more customers. However, it's key that in this relationship you lead, and do not allow yourself to be led. You should be the ones suggesting ideas and getting support in areas that are more of interest to you. A good technology or software company will expect this and will aid you in this kind of relationship, one in which customer service is central. And while it is true that most modern educational technology is designed with users in mind, your context is the key. Is the solution designed for general education, not specifically language? And if so, what needs to be adapted? Is it designed for a large institution, such as a university, whereas you are working at a small private language school? If so, how can you make it work to your needs, not the needs of the bigger, richer customer?

The implications for an effective ongoing training programme

Having said all that, we suggest that, as much as possible, training be led from within. The stages of technological change cycle we have presented means that there is a core team who are the experts and leaders of the change. This group understands the needs of the end users, because they are among those users, and they can also respond more easily to questions of the type "Can I do this?", because they are connected to the context and the need, and therefore understand how that would best be achieved. They approach the issue from the perspective of the teacher or other staff member, rather than from the perspective of the technology. In addition, if the core team previously described is made up of teachers (at least in part), they are professionally able to get their point across successfully. They understand both theoretically and instinctively how learning happens, and can genuinely support teachers and others in internalising the processes necessary to fully integrate new technology in their classrooms. Perhaps the key thing to remember when setting up training is that it needs to be constantly focussed on the needs of the end users (teachers and students, even parents where applicable), and your core team should be able to keep the training on track to fulfil that objective, hence providing a training programme that will satisfy the real and perceived needs of those being trained.

The other key thing to note is that this training should be an ongoing, iterative process that continues around a **cycle** and needs to be followed up on and added to. It is a dialogue and a conversation between 'trainer' and 'trainee', rather than information being simply passed from A to B.

Wedell (2009) describes the following set of understandings that teachers must gain through the process of training:

a. developing a deep understanding of what the aims of the change mean for classroom practice and why they are worth introducing
b. using their current level of understanding (with or without more expert help) to plan how to introduce new practices
c. trying out new practices with learners in the classroom
d. seeing what happens when doing so – obtaining explicit or implicit feedback from the learners, colleagues or a more expert 'coach'
e. going through many more cycles of (a) to (d), slowly developing a more complete personal understanding and personal confidence in practice through carrying it out again and again

If the stages of technological change cycle as described in this book have been followed to this point, then step (a) here has already been achieved. What follows in this part of the change process is a constant cycling from (b) to (d), which is carried out by the end users of the technological innovation with the support and involvement of those designated as trainers. The role of the trainer here is variously teacher, coach, mentor, listener, observer, feedback giver, researcher and more. There also need to be channels opened through which things learned by the various end users and trainers can be fed back into the system, such that other team members can learn from the experience. And of course, there may be occasions where some of those who begin the process as the users supported by trainers become in turn the experts who take on a training role.

Connected to this, and to steps (c) and (d), there is also the role of communities of practice in developing creative approaches and ideas making use of the technology. This is very often from where some of the most interesting and inventive uses of the technology will come.

Also, as part of Wedell's cycle there needs to be a parallel focus on observing and giving feedback to users on their implementation and use of the new technology. This is important, as it not only informs the type of training that needs to be included as the programme evolves, but also ensures timely feedback to users before they create any sort of fossilised bad practice. This process of observation and feedback helps ensure also that any user who is still uncomfortable using the new solution, or who may perhaps have been left out of the training or onboarding, can be trained appropriately and included in the ongoing process. This element of training is one which cannot be stand-alone, but rather is very intimately related to the training being provided as described above. Without this element, it will be much more difficult for leaders to determine the most appropriate next steps, and may keep end users' real needs out of the conversation when determining the ongoing cycle of training.

Putting this type of training into practice can be a real paradigm shift for stakeholders and leaders, and true to the model we have presented, requires constant reflection, feedback and support. The leaders need to listen and be present during the process, in order to determine the frequency and intensity with which the cycle repeats and is acted upon. For many, one continuous cycle during one established learning period (e.g. a semester) may be enough. Others may find that they only need to focus on this training cycle once a year. As users become more experienced and more engaged with the tools and the learning, the quantity and quality of the training needs may change.

The importance of leaders and involved stakeholders in this process is key to ensuring that the cycle is enacted fully, and that results and learnings are used to impact training as well as decisions.

Task 4.1: Personal experience of new technology

Think back to when you learned to use a new piece of technology in your personal or professional life.

1. How did you approach it?
2. Did you have any training?
3. What form did the training take?
4. How much recycling of things you learned did you have to go through before you were comfortable using the technology?
5. What kind of learning curve did you undergo? Did you find it easy to grasp at the start, but more difficult to get used to more complicated features, or did you find it quite hard to get started, but once you had begun learning, quite easy to pick everything up?
6. Do you feel that you have learned everything that is useful to you in this tool?

Now, think of a larger technological change that your organisation (past or present) went through.

1. What form did the training take?
2. Did the training follow any or all of the ideas mentioned above?
3. Was it a successful transition?
4. Why / Why not?

🔍 **Case study:** A successful training programme

A university language programme providing foundation year teaching to students entering RMIT (Royal Melbourne Institute of Technology), an English-medium university in Vietnam, decided to move to a new curriculum which included having a greater degree of blended instruction and online testing. Key to the change, it was clearly necessary to train the teachers (and the students) in the technology that was about to become a fundamental part of their work. The training was designed in-house, and was presented in step-by-step workshops – both face-to-face and online. The training started out as fairly minimal instruction on how to use a new LMS. Later, it evolved to include more practical workshops on using the LMS in the specific context and a knowledge 'toolkit', which consisted of practical activities testing the knowledge gained from both the face-to-face workshops and the online tutorials.

The biggest issue was found to be disparities in knowledge. Some teachers were proficient at using technology and could deal with the new processes easily, while some struggled, so the training given had to cater for a wide range of abilities. The same was true with the students; some had had access to technology their entire life, while others had only limited experience. So the training on offer had to successfully instruct technologically inexperienced teachers to a suitable level to have enough confidence to teach an inexperienced student to complete the tasks. But, at the same time, it also needed to confirm and extend the knowledge of teachers with technological experience without seeming patronising. As a result, self-paced online tutorials were incorporated into the training.

A feedback loop was created, so that as the training continued (for both teachers and students), things that had been learned could be used to adapt and improve the systems themselves, as well as the training materials and both the face-to-face and the online workshops. This was all guided and supported by the member of teaching staff charged with learning technology development. In addition, some teachers quickly became specialists and took on more responsibilities to help guide the development and integration of the changes.

While some of the less technologically experienced teachers gained confidence and understanding of the fundamentals, the more technologically confident teachers moved forward, and made suggestions and improvements both to the training materials and to the way that the technology was being used.

Stage 7: Monitoring and evaluating

Drawing up a **monitoring and evaluation plan** is a crucial part of any planning process, and should not be, as sadly it so often is, an afterthought. Through your objectives you have a clear idea of what you want to achieve in the change, so the starting point of your evaluation strategy is already in place.

The purpose of monitoring and evaluation

Broadly speaking the monitoring and evaluation plan fulfils the following functions:

- It clearly lays out the intended results of the change – in terms of both outputs and outcomes, where outputs (or deliverables) are the concrete changes that will be made, and outcomes (or impacts) are the less tangible effects of the change.
- It establishes a baseline measure of how things were before the change, against which we can measure its impact.
- It compares the ongoing results of the change with the hoped-for outcomes.
- It informs the manager of the indicators that they should watch for which will tell them to adjust the implementation (e.g. if a particular task is taking longer than expected or that more training is necessary).
- It suggests actions that can be taken in order to adjust the implementation of the change as and when necessary.

Questions to guide monitoring and evaluation

Quite simply, every action in the implementation plan can be evaluated. In some cases, that evaluation may be as simple as ticking off a task as done on a checklist. In others, some more in-depth evaluation techniques may be called for.

Some questions that you may be asking for **continuous evaluation** at different stages and in relation to different tasks include:

- Did the task get done?
- Did the task get done on time?
- Did the task get done to the required standard?
- What is the feedback from the different stakeholder groups?
- How do costs at this stage measure against our original budget?
- What obstacles were there?
- What do we need to learn from this stage for future stages?

There are many more, and, as you can see, some of these are simple and quantitative in nature, while others are much more in-depth and may need various types of research instruments.

At its simplest, a monitoring and evaluation plan answers five questions:

1. What are we going to evaluate?
2. When?
3. How will it be evaluated?
4. Who is responsible for evaluating it?
5. What will we do with the results of the evaluation?

A task to collect information via survey from key stakeholders, in the early stage of a project, for example, might be as simple as:

1. *(What to evaluate)* The number of people who responded to the survey
2. *(When)* By the assigned deadline on the project timeline
3. *(How)* Evaluated by counting responses
4. *(Who)* Evaluated by the project manager
5. *(What to do with the results)* If we have received fewer than 80%, follow up and personally ask others to respond

Whereas, having developed an online summative assessment test and had a pilot group of students take it, the evaluation may be a little more complex:

1. *(What to evaluate)* Did every student complete the test? Were there any problems with technology? Did they achieve the expected grades?
2. *(When)* After students have taken the test.
3. *(How)* By checking the students' test responses and results for problems, obtaining feedback on the test experience from students (via a feedback form), and comparing with same group's grades on a paper-based version of the test at the same level.
4. *(Who)* Collected by teachers and the project manager.
5. *(What to do with the results)* If there are significant variances, investigate and remedy. If the grading appears accurate, and the functionality was effective, then move on to the next stage of the project. Consider what back-up plans will be needed if any technological issues arose.

This fifth question is very important, as so often evaluation is done and then the results merely filed. Considering what actions to take is a key element of evaluation.

⚙ Task 4.2: Reflection on a change

Think about a change that you recently went through, or are currently going through, and answer these questions:

1. How was the monitoring and evaluation carried out?
2. Was the monitoring and evaluation fully and thoroughly planned before the change was begun?
3. Are there things you wish you had thought about before you began?
4. How did you act on the results of the evaluation(s)?

Celebrating successes

It is also very important to celebrate our successes. When a large change or project is underway it can be a long process from beginning to end. This can feel exhausting to those who are dealing with the change. In Kotter's highly influential 8-step change model (Kotter, 1996 – see panel below), "Create quick wins" is Step 6, and this is a key stage in the process.

⚙ Kotter's 8-step change model

One of the best-known models of change is that developed by John Kotter (1996). Kotter proposed an **8-step change model**, as seen here:

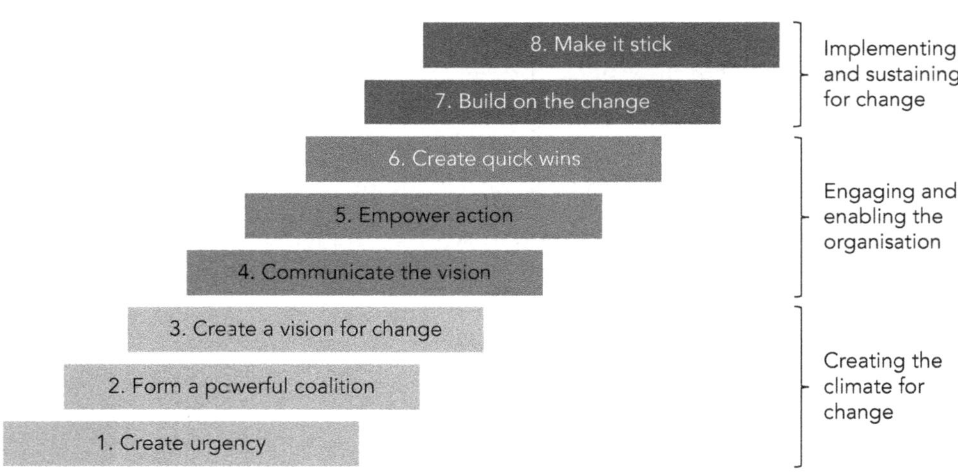

Figure 4.3: Kotter's 8-step change model

The successful change process, as proposed by Kotter, is as follows:

1. **Create urgency.** For change to be successful, it must be desired by everyone. This stage involves a clear rationale for making the change, and the involvement of some key stakeholders in 'selling' the need. It's not about sowing fear, but about having honest conversations which are convincing. The key people in the organisation must buy in to the change or, in Kotter's view, it will be impossible to make it work.
2. **Form a powerful coalition.** This is similar to the 'Teaming' phase in our model: bring together a core group of people, who may need to be involved through status, expertise, enthusiasm and political influence.
3. **Create a vision for change.** Build a clear vision that can be easily explained and 'sold', and build a strategy around that vision. The members of the core team need to be able to explain the vision clearly, concisely, and convincingly.
4. **Communicate the vision.** Connect everything to the vision and talk about it constantly. Address people's fears and concerns openly and directly And also make sure you (as leader) 'walk the talk', acting as you expect others to act.
5. **Empower action.** Remove any obstacles that are obstructing the change. These may be connected to resistance, which needs to be overcome through persuasion, or to processes and systems that seem to be getting in the way of the effective change process. Recognise those who are succeeding in acting upon the change.
6. **Create quick wins.** Make sure there are short-term targets, to encourage everyone that the change is working and things are moving along successfully towards the vision. These targets need to be achievable (short-term 'wins' that you don't reach will be demotivating!).
7. **Build on the change.** Don't declare victory too early, and ensure you keep looking forward. After success, make sure you look at what went well and how you can build on that (and also at what still needs to be done).
8. **Make it stick.** Make sure the change becomes part of the culture of the organisation, that the vision you identified at the beginning is now reality and that, again, this is referred to often. Remember the change, and the vision that lay beneath it, and also ensure that new staff are made aware of it as they are brought in.

If you have reached a clearly defined milestone in the process, perhaps piloting some online materials, or getting one whole level's curriculum rewritten to reflect a blended component, then mark the occasion. Hold a small event, bring cake, highlight the contributions of the various key players in getting to that point. Evaluation is not just about ticking stages off a list.

Sharing lessons learned and expanding uses

One of the outcomes of the monitoring and evaluation process may be a realisation that what is being introduced or changed can benefit other programmes or departments. For example, a language school that is part of a chain may be creating a successful innovation in their work which other schools in the chain could very much benefit from. Likewise, a university faculty might be able to support their colleagues in other faculties with the lessons they have learned through the introduction of some new technology.

Expanding on the success of the programme can allow you not only to implement or suggest similar projects to other identified needs, or gaps in the current procedures, but also, as a team, to draw from that same success for future programme decisions and to advocate for more resources and expansion in your own programmes. Building upon success is a key feature of building a strong and sustainable programme, and it's important to remember that a major piece of success (however that is defined) includes strong, documented processes, with clear procedures and outcomes. Even the most successful technological integrations have some 'bumps' along the way, and it is important to record the process and clearly and fairly outline the struggles. This will provide a pathway to success which you and your team can repeat and improve upon in other change processes in the future.

It's also important to note that this expansion need not necessarily be only internal to your organisation. The key people involved in the change, especially the core team, have the opportunity to support the wider profession, through writing articles, presenting at conferences, or even offering training sessions. The process is holistic in nature and provides unique opportunities for participants to leverage the experience in their own professional development and learning networks.

End-of-change evaluation

Evaluating the change – both as an ongoing process and at the end – ensures that everything has gone to plan and has been carried out effectively, as well as supports decisions as to whether the work can be leveraged in some other way and in some other context. Having done that evaluation, it remains to feed everything that has been learned back into the organisation. By this, we mean that the change model we have presented is a cycle, and a cycle that fits into an organisational culture that is constantly alert and questioning. The change that you have gone through will have, hopefully, created improvements in some ways of working. But, at the same time, it will have opened windows onto other possibilities and issues. Organisations are complex systems, and as with any complex system, any change, no matter how big or small, will have ripple effects that may or may not have been anticipated. Changes may reveal further gaps in technology (putting some coursework on a VLE, for example, may reveal the need for software plug-ins to allow for additional exercise types) or they may reveal blockages in the communication channels in the organisation itself.

Of course, it may not be that the change reveals gaps at all, but instead makes it clear that something can be built upon. The idea of appreciative inquiry, mentioned in Chapter 1, suggests that we take an asset-based approach to what we have and use it as a starting point. Perhaps your technological change has revealed a number of skills and talents among the staff, that you were previously unaware of. Can these skills be made even more use of?

Reflection on the process

Ensure that at the end of the change, you take time to reflect upon what you have learned, what you have gained and whether this reveals the next steps for the organisation or department. You could hold a final core team meeting, for example, at which you not only celebrate the success of the completed change, but also where the team can enter into an in-depth and structured team reflection. The points arising from this reflection can be listed and used to inform future projects.

Gibbs' (1988) **Reflective Cycle** (see Figure 4.4) can be used as a guide for this process, to ensure that the reflection is structured, and the maximum value obtained.

In this process, bring your team back together for the final project meeting and work through the different stages in this cycle. Start with 'Description'. Remind yourselves of all the stages you went through and the different things that happened along the way, including individual moments and longer actions or phases. In this stage, you should simply describe the things that occurred rather than commenting on them. The second element of the cycle is 'Feelings'. Think about how all of you as individuals felt at the different stages of the transition process. Was there also a general feeling in the project team and in the wider organisation? Were you all aware of what the others were feeling at these points? And how do you feel now, having reached the end of the process?

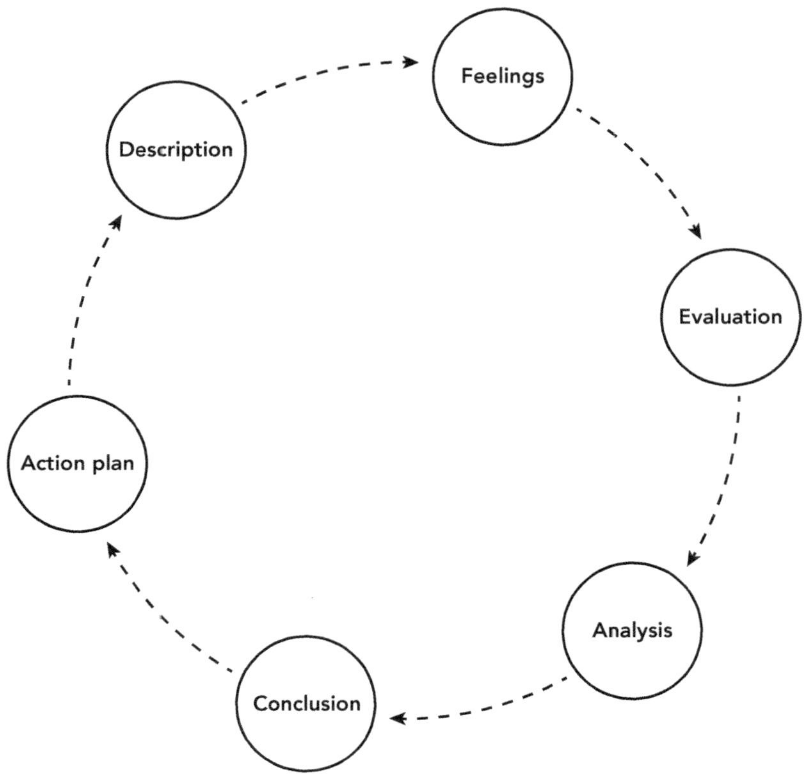

Figure 4.4: Gibbs' Reflective Cycle (Gibbs, 1988)

'Evaluation' is the next step, and here we mean evaluation of the process, not the technology itself. Ask the team what was good about the process, and also about what didn't go so well. Lead a discussion on the good and the bad, and also allow people to evaluate their own personal contributions to the process, and the final product. Encourage people to be as objective and honest as possible. The 'Analysis' step is about making sense of all that you have discussed so far, asking yourselves why certain things went well or went badly. You might want to review this book, for example, or any other models of change that you like, seeing if the literature can provide any insights into things that didn't go well, or things that went very successfully.

Finally, as a 'Conclusion', summarise and think about things you want to learn and to take away from this experience as individuals (for example, skills learned) and as a team (for example, ways of working together). And then, of course, discuss an 'Action plan' for future changes. What do we want to remember for next time? How can I develop the skills I have decided I need? How can we ensure that we take the positives from this experience and avoid the negatives next time around?

Going through the end-of-project reflection process will help the individuals, the project team, and the wider organisation to ensure that what can be learned from the process is captured and made into something of value.

Summary

In this chapter, we have looked at the implementation of the project plan. We've considered the ways that, in particular, training can be carried out to ensure that everyone is successfully served by it. In addition, we've thought about monitoring and evaluation – the ways that this can be carried out successfully and, importantly, the uses to which the evaluations can be put. Not only in terms of the ongoing change process itself, but also extending it, within and outside the organisation. Finally, we've discussed ways in which the whole process can be reflected upon and lessons learned.

 If you want to find out more...

Gibbs, G. (1988). *Learning by doing: A guide to teaching and learning methods.* Further Education Un t, Oxford Polytechnic.

This is a very influential book in education. In particular, the reflective cycle described here has been widely adopted by those studying, practising and teaching the skills of critical reflection.

Kirkpatrick, J. D., and Kayser Kirkpatrick, W. (2016). *Kirkpatrick's Four Levels of Training Evaluation.* Association for Talent Development.

Don Kirkpatrick's original *Four Levels of Training Evaluation* is the most widely used training evaluation model in the world. This book, by his son and daughter-in-law, extends and deepens the use of the model.

Tribble, C. (Ed.) (2012). *Managing change in English language teaching: Lessons from experience.* British Council.

This presents project management and change case studies from ELT contexts around the world, with commentary, and is recomended reading.

Wedell, M. (2009). *Planning for educational change: Putting people and their contexts first.* Continuum/Bloomsbury

This links educational policy and the management of change in various different contexts around the world, integrating theory and practice, and also includes a number of real-life case studies for analysis.

Conclusion

| Reviewing the cycle

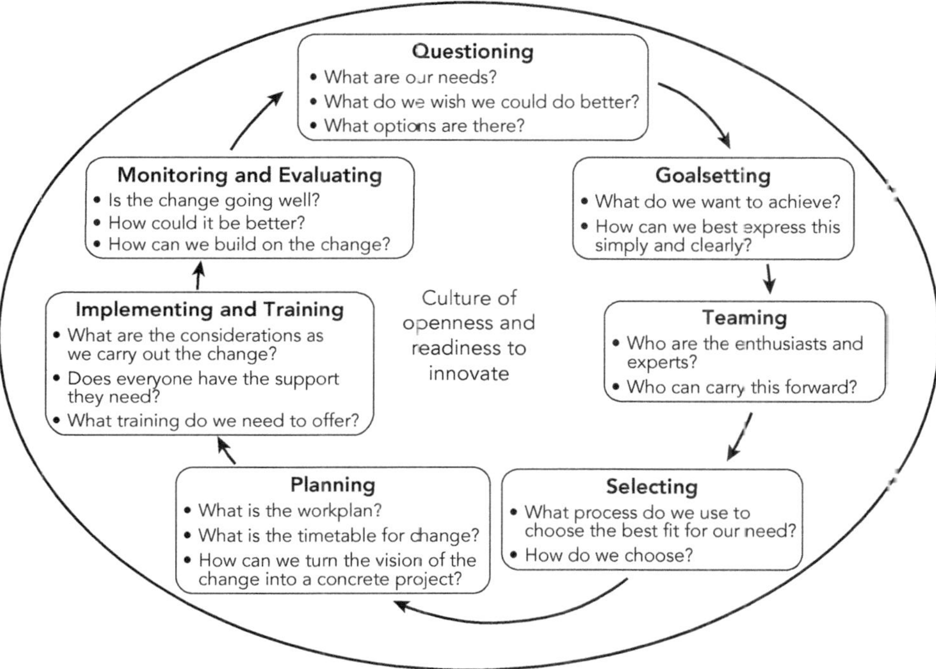

Figure 5.1: The stages of technological change

Modern technology has a huge amount to offer language education and the processes that facilitate the delivery of that education. As a leader, it is part of your role to remain up to date and to be aware of what is possible, what is happening elsewhere, and how your own organisation might be improved, as well, of course, of the learning of the students you serve.

Creating a culture of questioning and openness will allow these conversations to be heard, ensuring that your staff have a voice and that you are likely to be ready and able to move with the times and invest in the most effective and useful technological solutions that will support the work of your LTO. This doesn't mean, of course, that each time you will get it right, but the wisdom of crowds will ensure that a diverse set of viewpoints and insights will give you a good chance of choosing wisely, ensuring buy-in, and, as an added value, enhancing motivation.

"

Having opened up these dialogues and discussions, the steps presented in this book will, we hope, help you to lead the process of selecting the correct technology to meet your needs, and ensuring that it is the best fit possible, before planning the process of not only integrating the technology physically into your school (with related training and support), but also integrating it effectively into your curriculum (in the case of educational technology).

In the midst of this innovative school culture, ideas and questions rise to the surface, and those ideas can be captured and made use of as the beginning of the change process (**Step 1: Questioning**, see Chapter 1). After making sure that you have clearly outlined the goals of the change (**Step 2: Goalsetting**, see Chapter 1), the core team needs to be formed, of key players in the particular technological enhancement being considered (**Step 3: Teaming**, see Chapter 2). This team should work together to make clear the objectives of the project, and to use the SELECT model to choose the best possible technological option given all the various criteria, including cost (**Step 4: Selecting**, see Chapter 2).

Once the choice has been made, the next stage is to draw up a clear plan as to how this change will be introduced, and communicate this to everyone who is likely to be affected in any way (**Step 5: Planning**, see Chapter 3). Then the plan is carried out, ensuring that all the stages of the process are worked through – including any physical changes that may need to be made, all training and support for users, and the integration of the technology into the curriculum or standard office processes and procedures (**Step 6: Implementing and Training**, see Chapter 4).

Throughout, all the different aspects of the project should be monitored and evaluated, with any necessary changes to the plan made as and when they are needed. Finally, as the technology slots into the 'business as usual' of the LTO, the changes (expected and unforeseen) that it brings up will feed into the questioning section as the cycle begins again (**Step 7: Monitoring and Evaluating**, see Chapter 4).

Q **Case study:** Putting it all together

The owner and management team of Jantar-IH Split, a private language school in Croatia, decided that they wanted a system that could help them better manage the school. They wanted an integrated system which covered aspects of the work from student grades and registrations to finance and administration. A consultation with all the members of staff was launched, to get a sense of what everyone wanted and felt would make their job more effective, and also what were the administrative tasks that they felt were uninteresting yet time-consuming. From this process they built up a clear picture of what exactly they were looking for, what it would do, and how it would support the school (both as a business and as an educational establishment).

A core project team was then formed, and with the information gleaned from the consultation, they investigated the school management systems on the market and looked at the features and functionality of each one. Ultimately, they decided that none really fitted their needs – some were good for student management, others were good for business processes, but none really managed to integrate them all in the way that they had hoped.

As a result, the team decided that the way forward would be to build their own school management system. The school applied for, and was granted, funding via the European Fund for Regional Development. This funding covered approximately half of their costs and the rest was supplied by the school itself. With the money, they were able to upgrade the IT equipment at the school and, crucially, to fund a locally-hired full-time IT developer to help build the planned system.

Luckily, the school was able to free up the project leader to work full time on the new system, and over the next nine months he and the IT developer worked together to design, build and test the new system. Having the project leader work alongside the developer proved to be the key to the project's success. If the developer had just been given the specs and asked to develop the product, the back and forth would have taken much longer. Also, the end result would have been based on the developer's understanding of what was possible from previous experience, rather than building something that was truly innovative and which would genuinely meet the school's needs.

Throughout this process, the project leader went back and forth with staff in the school, demonstrating and testing out individual aspects of the system, gathering feedback and ensuring that the system would work for them. This also meant that staff were kept involved and could see that the project was progressing successfully.

When the software was completed, training was actually fairly minimal, since all staff members and other end users had been trialling and testing out the programme as it was being built. However, training workshops and online self-paced courses were still put together, with the support of the team, for use with staff hired after the implementation of the new system.

As the system rapidly became integral to the whole operation of the school – from grades, registers, exam results, financial systems and reminders to the database upon which the website was built – some gaps and flaws became apparent, but these were able to be reconciled quickly and easily.

So successful was the new system that the school decided to set up a new company to market the software to other private language schools of a similar size and profile. As it was a small team running a bespoke system, this was able to be a system specifically tailored to each school's needs. The original IT developer became the CEO of this new company, has a permanent staff of four, and the system has been purchased by a growing number of language schools in Europe, Asia, and South America. In addition to the financial benefits, the collaboration between schools that it created has meant a number of industry-specific software development projects across borders have been publicly and privately funded.

The Covid-19 crisis

During the writing of this book, the world was hit by the Covid-19 pandemic. As a result, nearly all language schools around the world were forced to confront technological change of one kind or another. The sudden shift from face-to-face to online teaching and learning meant that language school managers (as well as many others) had to urgently negotiate a huge change in the business and academic models that we had all become so familiar with. There are a number of lessons that we can learn from this in the general management of technological change in English language teaching. However, there are some features of this emergency change that are less useful in understanding the process of planned change.

In broad terms, there is a significant difference between **change management** and **crisis management**. To a large degree, what happened when traditional classrooms were shut down overnight, as was the case in many contexts, was about crisis management. There was an urgent need to make the shift to online teaching, with all that this involved in terms of technology, support, logistics, training, team building, curriculum design, assessment, and much more. What was achieved all over the world in all educational contexts, in no time at all, was nothing short of miraculous. Students, teachers, student support staff, tech support, and academic managers worked together to practically build something out of nothing. It was overwhelming, exhausting, supportive, compassionate, and imperfect.

Unlike the typical form of change management (like the kind described and suggested throughout this book), this change was unplanned (in some contexts schools had a week to change, in others a weekend, in a few slightly longer). There was no time for the coalition building or the analysis of potential options as presented here. But, on the other hand, there was also a lack of the resistance that comes along with most significant change processes.

Everybody at all levels understood that there were no other options and that we all had to get on with making the shift to emergency remote teaching. The other major difference was that we went into this change process seeing it as a temporary matter, something which was an emergency fix, keeping things together until we could revert to normal.

So, if it was a significantly different process, what did we learn about leading technological change?

1. **The value of communication**. Communication in a crisis is essential, but this is also true of a change process. Making sure that everyone is kept aware of what is happening, that they feel they understand the needs and the process, is crucial. People need to know both the big picture and the details. Schools and programmes which kept their staff informed and included throughout the initial stages of the crisis and beyond were ones that not only preserved the crucial relationships and sense of teamwork, but were also the ones that created the conditions for multi-directional communication, allowing them to be more agile and able to deal with the situation.

2. **The importance of support**. In any change process, teachers and other staff need support. Change presents problems, and everybody charged with implementing or acting on change needs help and support. In the pandemic situation, everyone needed support, not merely because of the huge nature of the change, but because they were dealing with the wider uncertainties of the situation and the potential isolation brought on by working from home. However, this level of support, contacting staff, listening to them, being aware of how they are coping with the change and where they seem to need help, is a crucial part of leading change.

3. **The power of reflecting in and on action**. The importance of constant monitoring and reflection about how we are doing, what can be adjusted, and where we are going is crucial to any change process, as we discussed in Chapter 4. In this case as there was very little planning time, we were not able to compare with a plan, but we were still able to reflect during the process. The reflective cycle presented at the end of Chapter 4 can and should be used at the end of the process of change, but also at points within the change. In an urgent unplanned change like the ones associated with the Covid-19 pandemic, this is doubly important, but it is also of great value in a more planned process.

4. **The paradox of technology**. Technology is surprisingly effective and versatile and can be used in ways that many of us had never imagined or trusted before. The forced migration to emergency remote teaching demonstrated to teachers, students, and academic managers alike that there are possibilities that many of us had not previously been aware

of, and that online teaching and learning can in fact be an effective approach. At the same time, and in seeming opposition to the first observation, many of the same people have also become acutely aware of the idea that, at least in language teaching, face-to-face learning spaces are preferable for a number of reasons, both pedagogical and social. It is not the place of this book to look into all that has been learned and will continue to be learned through this period, but a lot of research is being carried out and there is a lot of data to work with. Individual teachers and academic managers, as well as language schools themselves, will learn a lot by reflecting upon what they have been through and are continuing to go through. This experience may be beneficial in supporting and promoting future innovations, but it also may well be a block.

5. **The significance of organisational culture**. We began our model looking at the kind of organisational culture that allows change and ideas about innovation to "bubble up". A lot of what can be taken from the experience of the move to emergency remote teaching is not so much about the technology itself (although, of course, our experiences here will and do have a lot to teach us), but about what an open, trusting LTO looks like. For a period in early 2020, most such organisations that we are familiar with had these features. People listened to each other, ideas were shared and discussed, and everybody in the whole organisation recognised that they were all beginners and that all voices were, to an extent, equal.

While language programme managers within the context of Covid-19 worked to solve the educational crisis they were faced with, the principles of the planning process become important to return to, once we realise that online education, in many cases, is here to stay. Certainly, we have all been afforded the opportunity to feel the impact different uses of technology may have on our teaching, managing and evaluation of programmes. Technology became the substitute for the personalised contact of the face-to-face environment in teaching, and now many educators are faced with the reality of taking a step back and re-evaluating their programmes to determine which of these integrations should continue, take the place of others, or be discontinued once a new learning programme is established. Perhaps the technology implemented during times of crisis will help us move forward in ways we had previously thought undesirable or unnecessary, as we continue to evolve with language programmes in our increasingly globalised learning environment.

Final thoughts

We hope that the ideas presented in this book will help you in making the often difficult decisions connected to technological change. It may be worth reflecting on a change that you have already been involved in to see to what extent it followed the model presented here, and if there were differences, whether those missing steps might have resulted in a smoother change process. Likewise, if you are already engaged in leading some form of technological innovation in your LTO at the moment, think about where and how you can adjust it to this model. For any future change, we hope that this model will provide some clear direction, and also remove some of the uncertainty that comes from the seemingly endless options out there.

In the **Appendices** to this book, we have provided you with some tools that can be useful as you begin to make this kind of ongoing technological change management a part of your continued professional practice. These tools and checklists can provide easy reminders for you as you work through the steps of change management we have covered together, and can also be used to create rough drafts of your process and easily adaptable templates for use with stakeholders and formal reporting processes along the way.

Appendices

Appendix 1: Overview of the stages of technological change

Before you start

- [ ] Review (or create) the LTO's vision
- [ ] Review (or create) the LTO's long-range plan (goals to achieve)
- [ ] Review (or create) the LTO's operational plan (specific actions to take to achieve the goals of the long-range plan)
- [ ] Develop a culture of openness – encourage staff to come to you with ideas
- [ ] Support professional development, including the formation of communities of practice and participation in professional learning networks

Stage 1: Questioning

- [ ] Keep your eyes open to changes in the industry
- [ ] Conduct a SWOT analysis of your LTO
- [ ] Be open to ideas from others (teachers, students, parents, the marketing team, etc.)
- [ ] Evaluate the need for specific changes using force field analysis
- [ ] Think critically about potential changes and get others' opinions on ideas

→ See **Appendix 2: Identifying the drivers of change**

Stage 2: Goalsetting

- [ ] Be clear about the purpose of the change, what the change will achieve, and what the change will look like
- [ ] Communicate the details of any change promptly, clearly, and positively

Stage 3: Teaming

- [ ] Identify the people who will work with you to implement the change – this will probably include members of the management team, end users of the solution (including teachers), 'mavens' and 'salespeople', and the people who proposed the change
- [ ] Establish sub-goals and objectives for the project
- [ ] Plan how you will communicate with the various stakeholders

→ See **Appendix 3: Checklist for developing a communication plan**

→ See **Appendix 4: Communication guidelines**

Stage 4: Selecting

- [ ] Make sure that the objectives of the change are clear
- [ ] Establish a list of criteria that are important for the solution (including the issue of cost)
- [ ] Find some realistic solutions to evaluate in more depth
- [ ] Evaluate the solutions using the list of criteria you developed
- [ ] Pilot the best option (or options)
- [ ] Make a decision about the solution that will be used

→ See **Appendix 5: Technology evaluation questions**

→ See **Appendix 6: Guidelines for costing your project**

Stage 5: Planning

- [ ] Establish the resources and time available to implement the change
- [ ] Identify any potential obstacles
- [ ] Define the tasks that need to be completed to reach the goal
- [ ] Order the tasks – identifying any tasks that can only be done after the completion of another task
- [ ] Assign a person and deadline to each task
- [ ] Clarify the outputs and outcomes of the project
- [ ] Develop an overall schedule and plan (perhaps by creating a Gantt chart)
- [ ] Conduct a stakeholder analysis
- [ ] Conduct a risk assessment
- [ ] Develop mitigation strategies and contingency plans to deal with risks
- [ ] Devise a monitoring and evaluation plan

→ See **Appendix 7: Guidelines for project planning**

→ See **Appendix 8: Presentation planning and delivery guidelines**

→ See **Appendix 9: Decision tree for monitoring stakeholder feedback**

Stage 6: Implementing and training

- [ ] Decide who needs to be trained and what they need to be trained on (focus on the needs of end users)
- [ ] Decide who will do the training (both initially and in the long term)
- [ ] Establish the frequency and intensity of training cycles

- [ ] Have the trainers develop the training materials
- [ ] Ensure that feedback on the training and the needs of those being trained is paid attention to, and feeds back into the training cycle
- [ ] Look out for emergent experts who can train, mentor and support others

Stage 7: Monitoring and evaluating

- [ ] Decide what needs to be evaluated, how it can be evaluated, and how often
- [ ] Plan how and when you will celebrate successes
- [ ] Look for opportunities to share knowledge with others
- [ ] At the end of the project, reflect on the success of the project and the lessons learned

→ See **Appendix 10: Tips for successful change management**

Appendix 2: Identifying the drivers of change

When you need to make decisions about prioritising change, it's important to be clear on the drivers of these changes. A good way to do this is to create a succinct summary in the form of a table, which should also help ensure that everyone has this information to hand to aid in decision-making. This table can be added to as the project progresses and additional changes need to be considered.

When placing changes into the table, you need to consider two choices about the drivers of change:

- **Is it an essential change or a desirable change?** An essential change is one that is necessary to ensure the continuance of the programme. On the other hand, a desirable change is something that could improve your programme or provide your LTO with a competitive advantage, but not necessarily a change that would impact the continuance of the programme directly.

- **Is it an externally-driven change or an internally-driven change?** An externally-driven change comes from forces outside the institution or the programme over which you have no control – such as a curriculum update by the ministry of education, or a change to the technology you are using by the provider. An internally-driven change is one motivated by the people within your institution – for example, changes inspired by student or teacher feedback or changes that you wish to make to your programme.

Here is an example:

Table A2.1: An example of the drivers of change

	Essential	Desirable
Externally-driven	• State-mandated curricular update to the programme must be put into effect • Current platform provider will begin to phase out certain functions	• Parents have requested access to grade reports • Other schools within your direct competition have begun to use programmes with voice recognition technology • Other departments in the institution request English programmes integrate career-specific language into their courses
Internally-driven	• Classroom material is more than five years old and needs to be replaced • New programmes are being introduced and need online material	• Teachers want faster reporting tools • Students want more attractive platform content

The highest priority changes are likely to be the essential externally-driven changes, as these are the things that you have to do but have no control over. The essential internally-driven changes are the next most important ones – as these are internally driven you may have more control over when these changes are made. The desirable changes should be your third priority. They need to be considered in terms of both the effort required and the impact that they will have. It usually makes sense to prioritise the ones that will require less effort but have a big impact, and additional changes within the desirable range can be implemented if time and resources allow.

Appendix 3: Checklist for developing a communication plan

Good communication is essential for ensuring that your project stays on track and you have continued support and buy-in from stakeholders and participants in the process. Use the checklist below to help you plan how you will communicate with the wider group.

☐ 1. **Decide if the stakeholders need to meet as a full group, or in several smaller groups.** What is the most efficient way to ensure stakeholders receive the information they need, and how can you keep communication most effective? Should meetings be project-wide and include all stakeholders, or is it more effective to break stakeholders into smaller group meetings?

☐ 2. **Determine the frequency with which you will call working meetings with the full stakeholder group and keep a very clear calendar commitment to ensure maximum participation**. When establishing dates for update meetings, it's best to agree a regular day and time for the duration of the project so that this time is always booked out for everyone. However, if you need to schedule individual meetings, keep communication efficient by using online voting tools or calendar tools to find the most suitable times. After a meeting has been scheduled, make sure that all attendees are sent an agenda for the meeting in advance and avoid rescheduling the meeting unless absolutely necessary. If the meeting has to be moved, communicate the change in a timely manner and make sure stakeholders are given enough notice, so they can make any changes necessary to their own agendas.

☐ 3. **Clarify the frequency with which the LTO leadership require updates, and the best method to ensure their engagement.** Do they prefer an online meeting or a face-to-face session? Do they require information sent beforehand or do they prefer you to present information in the meeting?

☐ 4. **Establish a contingency plan for communication, if urgent challenges are encountered along the path to implementation.** How and through which medium can you count on communication with leadership? What communication tools will you use with your stakeholders to ensure they have a direct pathway to discuss these challenges with you as leader?

Appendix 4: Communication guidelines

As you begin work with your stakeholders and representatives, it is important to have clear, consistent and focussed communication about your progress on the project. This communication may be in the form of reports, memos meeting notes, emails, texts, or messages through online project management tool communications. Whatever the format, the importance of clear communication applies to all. If your communication is not clear, it could result in misunderstandings or even prevent the project from advancing. For example, if the primary stakeholders don't feel they consistently receive the updates they require to keep sending funding, this could lead to them putting a hold on funding or even cancelling support for the project.

The following guidelines can help you to communicate clearly and avoid these kinds of problems:

1. **Keep objectives clearly defined and at the top of each communication as you move through your project.** This will help with organisation and serve as key reminders for stakeholders about which stage and outcomes you are currently delivering on.

2. **Use bulleted summaries and include very clear impact implications.** These include what each element may represent in terms of budget, staff, time, outcomes, etc., so that each element you communicate is fully supported with the specific resources and major impacts your key stakeholders need to keep 'top of mind'.

3. **Send the information using a variety of mediums, to ensure all stakeholders receive the information.** You may want to send both an email and a group text notifying them of the more detailed email, or perhaps send an update in your online project management platform and a reminder email to check the information.

4. **Tailor the message to suit the interests of the stakeholder group you are communicating with.** Make sure the information that each group is mostly like to need (or that you need their thoughts on) is either highlighted or put first in your communication to this group.

5. **Put the most important information and main points at the beginning of your message, and supply more detailed information later on in the communication.** This allows busy stakeholders to stay up to date about the project and be aware of any key issues without having to review all the information until they have the time or need to do so. Remember that many stakeholders will be non-academic, and their approach will likely be to review key points and only focus on the details when needed.

6. **In written communication, include simplified pie charts, graphs, pictures, etc. that outline main points where appropriate.** Presenting information visually can help stakeholders to process the information. However, don't include lots of detail. Simplify charts and graphs and highlight any new or important information that you want stakeholders to be aware of.

7. **Where appropriate, include references to additional information or details (e.g. data from research, related research papers).** These can be annotations but will allow for stakeholders to get more detail if they need it.

8. **Highlight next steps and action points with deadlines.** Make sure everyone receiving the communication knows what (if anything) is expected of them and by when this action should be completed. You could also include recommendations for how to effectively use the information you are sharing.

Appendix 5: Technology evaluation questions

When brainstorming criteria to evaluate potential solutions, it can be hard
to remember all the different issues that you need to consider. This list of
suggested evaluation questions provides some ideas to use as a starting point.
The list is divided into three top-level categories: institutional considerations,
academic considerations, and sustainability considerations. Brainstorming
questions under these three top-level categories can be a good place to start
when thinking of topics and criteria.

Institutional considerations

- **Reporting**

  - Does this tool adapt to the institutional reporting needs?
  - Is data available and accessible as well as being safe for storing and
    providing a high level of validity for analysis?

- **Security**

  - Does the tool provide security settings which are adaptive to the
    requirements of the institution?
  - Is there any danger that student or staff data could be compromised?
  - Is there any danger that it will leave the organisation open to any
    form of attack or other vulnerability?

- **Ease of implementation**

  - Does the institution have the capacity to implement (with or without
    appropriate support)?
  - Are there infrastructure considerations (spaces, materials, etc.) that
    need to be arranged before implementation?

Academic considerations

- **Ease of use**

  - Does the tool provide enough support and consistent, user-friendly
    elements that facilitate use by all end users (teachers, students and
    admin staff)?

- **Content**

  - Is the content level and culture appropriate?
  - Is there enough content to fulfil expectations?
  - Can it be personalised for the institution, courses, and students?
  - Is the content compatible with the programme?

- **Assessment**
  - Are there sufficient tools available within the solution to provide a basis for assessment?
  - Does the tool provide assessment options appropriate for the desired outcomes?
  - Are there opportunities for students to receive feedback and automated assessment?
  - Do teachers receive enough information to correctly assess student use and learning?

- **Objectives**
  - Are the desired outcomes and objectives included in the solution or is it possible to personalise, to ensure objectives are obtainable?

Sustainability considerations

- **Cost/Budget**
  - Are the costs associated appropriate for both the institution and the users?
  - Are there associated maintenance and hosting charges the institution is willing to maintain?
  - Is there an institutional commitment to the long-term budget impact the solution could have for hosting, maintenance, upgrades, training, etc.?
  - Is new equipment required and easily acquired?
  - Is the institution prepared with space and budget to house new equipment?
  - Will there be additional costs to students for equipment?
  - Are there any opportunity costs?

- **Accessibility**
  - Is the tool easily accessible to end users?
  - Is there enough information and guidance available, and is the design accessible for all kinds of users?

- **Scale and longevity**
  - Is this solution scalable to meet the potential growth of the programme?
  - Can it provide more than a short-term solution for programme objectives?
  - Is it applicable (potentially) to other areas or programmes, in order to harness and take advantage of student success?

- **Training**
  - Is sufficient training available for all teachers and end users in the institution?
  - Is the training adapted to the timing and expectations of the institution?
  - Are spaces, materials and budget available to cover training needs?
  - Is follow-up training and support available?

- **Impact**
  - Can the technology be used to build upon its success?
  - Is there a possibility it will become irrelevant?
  - Are elements of the solution applicable to other areas of the institution?
  - Are there elements that improve efficiency and effectiveness in programme administration?

- **Partnership and prestige**
  - Is the provider of the solution willing to work with you and the institution in a continuous, supportive manner?
  - Will they provide the customer support functions you are looking for?
  - Is communication with the provider sufficient and are there possibilities to grow together in the relationship?

Appendix 6: Guidelines for costing your project

The questions below are to help the project team to make an estimate of costs. This is not meant to be an exercise in accountancy, and the team is not expected to have any great financial skills, but it is useful for them to be able to make a reasonably good estimate of costs.

Direct costs

Hardware. What hardware needs to be bought for this? (computers, projectors, interactive whiteboards, etc.). How many and at what cost? How soon will they need to be replaced?

Software. What software needs to be purchased? How many licences do we need? Is this a one-off payment or is it an annual licence fee?

Connectivity and infrastructure costs. Do we need to buy any other equipment or services, such as servers, cabling, routers, switchers, wireless access points, internet access, etc.?

Maintenance and personnel costs. Do we need to hire extra personnel for this project, either on a long-term contract or for any one-off tasks (such as installation, training, support, etc.), or will we be able to take care of this in-house?

Will we be required to purchase or lease any special tools, or high-cost replacement parts (e.g. projector bulbs)?

Renovation costs. Do we need to repurpose and/or rewire any rooms? Will this change involve the creation of special labs or other dedicated rooms or areas?

Professional development costs

What PD needs will we have for this? How much training? How much support? Can this be offered in-house? If in-house, how much time will those charged with delivering the training/support need to invest in preparing the training, and how many hours of training will be needed (see below)?

Staff hours costs

Roughly how many hours of in-house staff time will be needed to make this change?

- Project team / Project management – number of person-hours
- Professional development delivery – number of person-hours
- End users – number of person-hours of training time needed

Opportunity costs

Will the staff hours mentioned above take away from our ability to do other income–generating things such as teaching or – long-term – curriculum development?

If rooms are to be repurposed, how much income do those rooms currently generate?

Estimated financial benefits from the project

Time. How much time will be saved by using the new system when it is finally integrated into our systems (i.e. person-hours every month)?

Marketing benefits. Will the new technology be used for marketing purposes? What are the estimated effects on marketing?

Other income. Will the innovation generate any other income?

Costs of inaction. What would be the costs of *not* making this change?

Appendix 7: Guidelines for project planning

Use these questions to help list the various elements of your project as you go through the cycle. Having a clear list in this format will help you remain on top of the project as a whole, as well as enabling you to communicate clearly. Answer the following questions as clearly and concisely as possible. The more effectively you can do that, the easier you will find it to communicate to others.

1. What is the need/gap?

2. What is the overall goal? (solution to the problem identified in (1))

3. What is/are the objective(s)? (Make sure they are SMART(ER).)

4. a. What obstacles do you anticipate?
   b. What strategy do you have for avoiding or dealing with those obstacles?

5. a. Who are the key stakeholders (or stakeholder groups)?
   b. In each case:

   - What are their interests?
   - What are their perceived attitudes?
   - What do they need to do in order for the change to be successful?
   - How could you approach them and work with them (meet their needs / respond to their concerns / get what you need)?

   → Use a stakeholder analysis grid similar to Tables 3.3–3.5 to guide you here.

6. a. What are all the steps you need to accomplish to get to the goal? (Make a complete list)
   b. For each step:

   - When will it be done by?
   - Who is responsible for it?
   - Who else will be involved?
   - Which steps can be considered important milestones?

   → Create a Gantt chart to help visualise the steps and the timetable to complete them (see Figure 3.1 for an example).

7. How will you monitor and evaluate each step?
   a. What are you going to evaluate?
   b. When?
   c. How will it be evaluated?
   d. Who is responsible for evaluating it?
   e. What will you do with the results of the evaluation?

Appendix 8: Presentation planning and delivery guidelines

Use these guidelines to help you effectively present information to others – whether that is a five-minute chart or a long formal presentation.

In the days leading up the presentation

- **Hold a workshop with the project team to do a practice run-through of your presentation.** This allows the team to be involved in the specifics of what will be presented and ensure that there are no questions you are unprepared to answer. During this workshop, make sure all roles for the presentation are clear, including being very clear who will lead the process and who will take notes about questions and required actions.

- **Ask any stakeholders directly involved in delivering the presentation to participate in the workshop** and provide critical feedback on the overall form, content and feel of the presentation. If no stakeholders will be giving the presentation, invite some to participate in workshops to ensure they are happy with the format of the presentation.

- **Draft the supporting documents** (e.g. the slides or report) that will serve as the basis for the presentation and ensure that all participating stakeholders receive a copy in advance. Encourage them to review this material ahead of the presentation.

- **Follow up with stakeholders to ensure they have received the supporting documents, and send a short agenda** several days to a week before the event. This will allow for their feedback and time for any changes they request to your presentation or the activities you plan to do as you review information.

- **Confirm the arrangements for your meeting** (time, place, materials and technology needed for the presentation) with the site manager and anyone presenting during the meeting, at least one day before you present.

- **Stick as closely to the timing of your presentation as possible**. Remember that as well as respecting other people's time, it is also important for clarity that you plan for the time you have. Preparing a 35-slide presentation for a half-hour meeting will not allow you to provide clear, defined information to participants. Always plan and practice your presentation for the specific amount of time you have. Make sure you know how to shorten your presentation if you need to, and as you present, stick as closely as possible to the timing you practised.

On the day of the presentation

- **Arrive slightly early** (with previously granted permission if using a shared or executive space) to ensure the setup is correct and technology is functioning as desired.

- **Welcome stakeholders and make sure they are aware of the timeline of the meeting.** Indicate where they may find water, restrooms or office supplies (if needed), etc.

- **Provide a short overview of your presentation as you begin, and define when and how you can open the floor for questions and input.** You may want to allow stakeholders to ask questions and give their feedback during your presentation. If so, build space or pauses into your presentation to allow for interruptions in a way that does not interrupt the flow. If you are not comfortable with interruptions, or your presentation is best given fully before receiving questions or responses, make sure you explain that questions should wait until the end. Be prepared to give an overview of other stages of the process or answer questions about them – even if these stages are not the focus of your presentation. (Have notes on hand to help you do this.)

- **Provide a short summary of main points to close your presentation.** These quick 'take-aways' will allow you to keep the most important information top-of-mind for the stakeholders. You can also refer back to these points when you begin your next presentation as an easy way to recap the progress made so far.

- **Thank your stakeholders before they leave**.

After the presentation

- **Email the attendees the next day to thank them for their time and to share a brief bulleted list of the most important points covered.** If any questions were left unanswered during the presentation, you can provide further information in this email. You should also invite stakeholders to ask any further questions they have as they review, think about and work with the information you provided during the presentation/workshop.

- **Review your own performance and flag the elements you can improve for your next presentation.** Invite comments from your team and keep notes to help you plan your next presentation.

Appendix 9: Decision tree for monitoring stakeholder feedback

As you work with your team and comply with institutional requests for communication and feedback, it is important to ensure you are effectively reaching all the stakeholders in the process. This can become complex, depending on the project itself and the number of stakeholders. The decision tree below can help you remain focussed and ensure you are keeping stakeholder considerations in mind moving through the process. Ask yourself the following questions and follow the answer arrows below to make sure you are effective in this continuous process of feedback.

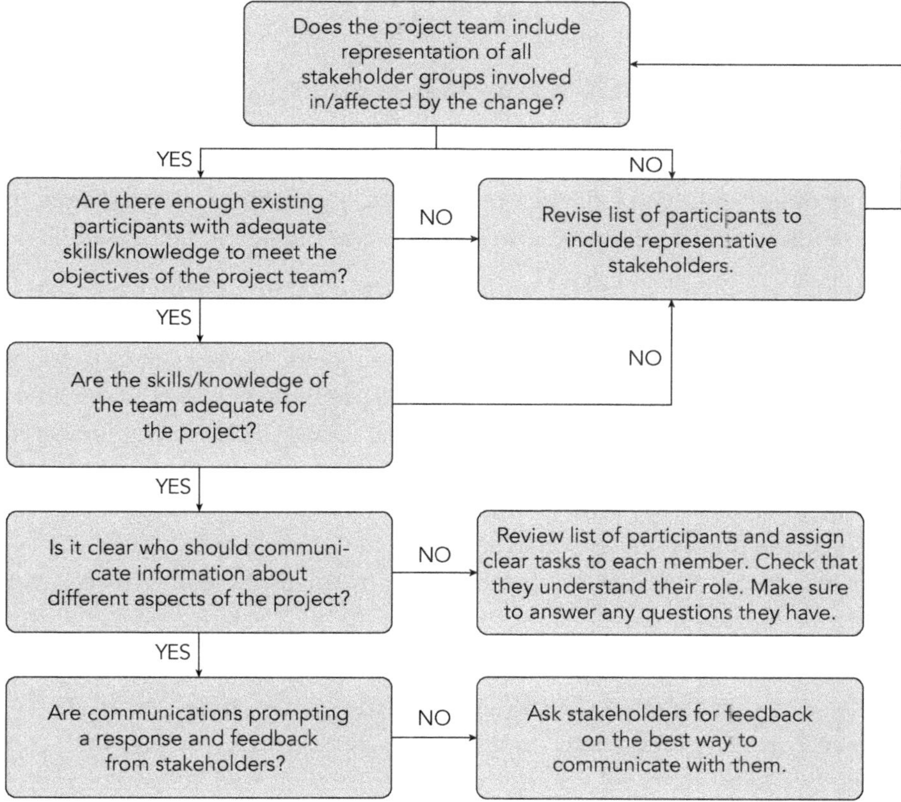

Figure A9.1: Decision tree for monitoring stakeholder feedback

Appendix 10: Tips for successful change management

As you begin the process of change management in your projects and institutions, it's important to remember that this may be an entirely new way of working for you and/or for others around you, and for some of those you may hope or expect to participate. As such, this is a process that needs nurturing within the institution in order to best assure success and continuity. While the process will need to be tailored for your specific circumstance, and likely adapted and modified as it progresses and grows, there are some fundamental steps that can help you in that process. The following may serve as some quick reminders for things to work on as you work through the process of integrating technology through the lens of sustainable change management.

1. **Keep the stakeholders' perspectives as primary points of consideration.** Remember that as you determine key factors in technology that may help you reach the objectives (learning, financial, teaching, outcomes, etc.), you will need to continually pull your stakeholders in to the conversation and remind them the process requires their input.

2. **Keep context as a central point of the discussion as you consider your options.** The perfect tool to satisfy one element of the project may in fact be the worst solution for another element. You may have to make some compromises in order to find the appropriate solution. There are many cases of tools integrated for the right reasons which simply won't be successful in a specific setting. For example, a platform which could provide teachers with the 'perfect solution' for the proposed learning outcomes may simply be unaffordable, whereas a cheaper tool simply may not have the right features to be of any impact. Keeping the context central to your discussions is crucial for striking a balance when choosing the best solution.

3. **Keep in mind that stakeholders will often be focussed on their own interests.** These may include financial concerns, institutional politics, specific responsibilities connected to their role, or other issues directly and indirectly connected to the project. Having a clear picture of these will allow you to understand how they may affect any resistance or support you may find from stakeholders as you work through the process of change.

4. **Consider the role of evaluation.** How will the technology be evaluated and what are you hoping to achieve? How will you and the process of integration be evaluated? Knowing that you will be appropriately responsible for outcomes is important to keep in mind, and building

a plan for evaluation, both continual as well as a final evaluation of
the completed project, during the process can help decrease any fear or
concern around retribution. Take some time to complete an evaluation
plan, which will help you review your process and the decisions taken.

5. **Bring in existing research and perspective on all the tools and
   approaches to technology integration as you begin the project.**
   While no one should expect dissertation-level research, having factual
   and anecdotal research around the elements you are evaluating can
   provide useful information to share with stakeholders and provide
   background knowledge and inspiration.

6. **Seek out negative comments or reviews of the technology you are
   considering.** Fully educating yourself on both the pros and cons of the
   situation means you are better prepared to answer questions and concerns
   from stakeholders. Besides, knowing about the limitations of a particular
   piece of technology may inspire solutions that improve the overall
   offering.

7. **Identify any wider implications this project may have.** Can the
   project serve any other offices within your organisation? Is this something
   you could share across your professional network? Could you participate
   in wider projects related to the same type of technology integrations?
   Considering these possibilities from the start can help you get the most
   you can out of the experience.

8. **Plan the schedule with enough time and resources for you to
   both work on the project and complete the other tasks that you
   normally do in your role.** It's important that the amount of time that
   you have to spend on your different responsibilities is clear both to you
   and to your leadership, so that expectations can be managed accordingly
   and additional resources found if necessary.

9. **Keep your stakeholders in the loop and use their feedback to guide
   you through the process**. Don't be afraid to take a step back or push
   pause if need be. Remember this is a process, and as such, trial and error
   may be a part of ensuring success.

References

Amabile, T., and Kramer, S. (2011). *The progress principle: Using small wins to invoke joy, engagement, and creativity at work.* Harvard Business Review Press.

Belbin, R. M. (2010). *Team Roles at Work* (2nd Edition). Routledge.

Bennett, N., and Lemoine, G. J. (2014, August 01). *What VUCA really means for you.* Harvard Business Review. https://hbr.org/2014/01/what-vuca-really-means-for-you

Blosch, M., and Fenn, J. (2018). *Understanding Gartner's hype cycles.* Gartner. https://www.gartner.com/en/documents/3887767/understanding-gartner-s-hype-cycles

Brush, T., and Saye, J. (2009). Strategies for preparing preservice social studies teachers to effectively integrate technology: Models and practices. *Contemporary Issues in Technology and Teacher Education, 9*(1), 46–59. https://www.learntechlib.org/primary/p/28300/

Buckingham, D. (2007). *Beyond technology: Children's learning in the age of digital culture.* Polity Press (Wiley).

Cummings, S., Bridgman, T., and Brown, K. G. (2015). Unfreezing change as three steps: Rethinking Kurt Lewin's legacy for change management. *Change Management, 69*(1), 33–60. https://doi.org/10.1177/0018726715577707

Edmondson, A. C. (2012). *Teaming: How organizations learn, innovate, and compete in the knowledge economy.* Jossey-Bass.

Education Review Office. (2018). *Leading innovative learning in New Zealand schools.* https://ero.govt.nz/our-research/leading-innovative-learning-in-new-zealand-schools-april-2018

Florida Center for Instructional Technology. (2019). *Technology Integration Matrix.* https://fcit.usf.edu/matrix/matrix/

Fullan, M. (2001a). *Leading in a Culture of Change.* Jossey-Bass.

Fullan, M. (2001b). *The New Meaning of Educational Change* (3rd Edition). Teachers College Press.

Gibbs, G. (1988). *Learning by doing: A guide to teaching and learning methods.* Further Education Unit, Oxford Polytechnic.

Gladwell, M. (2000). *The tipping point: How little things can make a big difference.* Little, Brown.

Greenleaf, R. K. (2002). *Servant leadership: A journey into the nature of legitimate power and greatness* (25th Anniversary Edition). Paulist Press.

Heath, C., and Heath, D. (2011). *Switch: How to change things when change is hard.* Random House.

Iarocci. J. (2017). *Servant leadership in the workplace: A brief introduction.* Cairnway.

Keane, T., Keane, W. F., and Blicblau, A. S. (2016). Beyond traditional literacy: Learning and transformative practices using ICT. *Educational and Information Technologies, 21,* 769–781. https://doi.org/10.1007/s10639-014-9353-5

Kirkpatrick, J. D., and Kayser Kirkpatrick, W. (2016). *Kirkpatrick's Four Levels of Training Evaluation.* Association for Talent Development.

Kolb, L. (2017). *Learning first, technology second: The educator's guide to designing authentic lessons.* International Society for Technology in Education.

Kotter, J. P. (1996). *Leading Change.* Harvard Business School Press.

Lewin, K. (1943). Defining the field at a given time. *Psychological Review, 50*(3): 292–310.

Project Agency. (n.d.). *Stakeholder analysis template.* http://ronrosenhead.co.uk/wp-content/uploads/2008/06/templates1.pdf

Puentedura, R. R. (2009). *As we may teach: Educational technology, from theory into practice.* http://www.hippasus.com/rrpweblog/archives/000025.html

Roddy, C., Amiet, D. L., Chung, J., Holt, C., Shaw, L., McKenzie, S., Garivaldis, F., Lodge, J. M., and Mundy, M. E. (2017). Applying best practice online learning, teaching, and support to intensive online environments: An integrative review. *Frontiers in Education, 2*(1). https://doi.org/10.3389/feduc.2017.00059

Rogers, E. M. (2003). *Diffusion of Innovations* (5th Edition). Free Press / Simon and Schuster.

Senge, P. M. (1990). *The fifth discipline: the art & practice of the learning organization.* Doubleday/Currency.

Spears, L. C. (Ed.) (1998). *Insights on leadership: Service, stewardship, spirit. and servant-leadership.* Wiley.

Tomlinson, B. (Ed.) (2013). *Developing Materials for Language Teaching* (2nd Edition). Bloomsbury.

Tuckman, B. W. (1965). Developmental sequence in small groups. *Psychological Bulletin, 63*(6), 384–399.

Viney, D. (2005). *The Intranet Portal Guide.* Mercury Web Publishing London.

Wedell, M. (2009). *Planning for educational change: Putting people and their contexts first.* Continuum/Bloomsbury.

Wenger, E. (1998). *Communities of practice: Learning, meaning, and identity.* Cambridge University Press.